DISCO

1 Find a time when you can read the Bible each day

2 Find a place where you can be quiet and think

4 Ask God to help you understand what you read

3 Grab your Bible and a pencil or pen

5 Read today's Discover page and Bible bit

6 Pray about what you have read and learned

We want to...

- Explain the Bible clearly to you
- Help you enjoy your Bible
- Encourage you to turn to Jesus
- Help Christians follow Jesus

Discover stands for...

- Total commitment to God's Word, the Bible
- Total commitment to getting its message over to you

Team Discover

Martin Cole, Nicole Carter, Rachel Jones, Kirsty McAllister, Alison Mitchell, André Parker, Ben Woodcraft
Discover is published by The Good Book Company, Blenheim House, 1 Blenheim Rd, Epsom, Surrey, KT19 9AP, UK.
Tel: 0333 123 0880; Email: discover@thegoodbook.co.uk UK: thegoodbook.co.uk
North America: thegoodbook.com Australia: thegoodbook.com.au NZ: thegoodbook.co.nz

How to use Discover

Here at Discover, we want you at home to get the most out of reading the Bible. It's how God speaks to us today. And He's got loads of top things to say.

We use the New International Version (NIV) of the Bible. You'll find that the NIV and New King James Version are best for doing the puzzles in Discover.

The Bible has 66 different books in it. So if the notes say…

Read Numbers 1 v 1

…turn to the contents page of your Bible and look down the list of books to see what page Numbers begins on. Turn to that page.

"Numbers 1 v 1" means you need to go to chapter 1 of Numbers, and then find verse 1 of chapter 1 (the verse numbers are the tiny ones). Then jump in and read it!

Here's some other stuff you might come across…

WEIRD WORDS

Daffnatle
These boxes explain baffling words or phrases we come across in the Bible.

Think!
This bit usually has a tricky personal question on what you've been reading about.

Action!
Challenges you to put what you've read into action.

Wow!
This section contains a gobsmacking fact that sums up what you've been reading about.

Pray!
Gives you ideas for prayer. Prayer is talking to God. Don't be embarrassed! You can pray in your head if you want to. God still hears you! Even if there isn't a Pray! symbol, it's a good idea to pray about what you've read anyway.

Coming up in Issue 8...

Numbers: Counting on God

Ever been on a loooong journey... so long that you started complaining?

We join the Israelites on a *really* long journey from Egypt (where they were slaves) to Canaan — the amazing land God has promised to give them.

But there's a problem. Even after God has done so much for them, the Israelites *keep on* complaining because they don't really trust Him. So God takes them on a 40-YEAR DETOUR to teach them a lesson.

We'll read all about it in the book of Numbers (and we'll take a quick peak at Deuteronomy too). This journey is long but never boring. Brace yourself for a super spy mission, an invasion of poisonous snakes and even a talking donkey!

John: The end for Jesus?

We'll tune in as John, one of Jesus' closest friends, gives us a first-hand account of three days that changed history for ever.

This stuff is seriously shocking and sad — Jesus is betrayed by one mate and abandoned by another. He's cruelly tortured and laughed at and executed, even though He's totally innocent! But John shows us how it was all part of God's plan to rescue us from sin. And Jesus chose to go through it because he loves us so so much!

And there's a twist in the tale for Jesus' friends three days later... read John to grab a front row seat on the action!

Romans: Only one way

Romans is a letter from the apostle Paul to Christians in Rome, Italy.

But Paul's not interested in the perfect pizza recipe. The only thing on his mind is the gospel — the good news about Jesus! And Paul wants to tell the Romans all about it.

But before Paul can get to the good news, he hits us with the bad news. Humans have a big problem: sin. But God has an even bigger solution... the gospel!

Ready to roll?
Then turn this way...

Numbers: Counting on God

**Numbers
1 v 1-46**

*The Israelites
were God's
special people.*

*God used Moses
to lead them out
of Egypt, where
they had been
treated badly as
slaves (we read
all about it in the
last few issues of
Discover).*

It's over a year since the Israelites escaped from Egypt. Now it's time to see how strong they are. They will be fighting battles on the way into **Canaan** — the country God promised to give them.

So in the special meeting tent, God told Moses what to do.

Read Numbers 1 v 1-4

Complete God's instructions. The answers are in the wordsearch.

T	W	E	L	V	E	Q	H	A
W	W	D	O	S	Z	G	E	J
Z	G	E	P	D	M	J	A	R
N	F	R	N	R	Y	O	D	S
C	N	K	L	T	R	I	B	E
F	A	M	I	L	Y	H	K	R
B	R	S	H	F	Q	B	U	V
A	M	E	N	P	M	C	W	E
L	Y	X	T	F	I	G	H	T

**Count the m _en___
aged t_wenty_ and
over, who are able to
f _ight___ (v3).**

**Get one man from each
t_ribe___ to help you. He
should be the h_ead__ of a
f_amily_ (v4).**

If you want to read all the details, they're in **verses 5-43**.

Now read verses 44-46

**So with the help of Aaron
and the t _welve___ family
leaders, they found that
the number of men able
to s_erve____ in Israel's
a_rmy__ was 603,550
(v44-46).**

What an army! But they'd be totally useless unless they **followed God's orders** (as we'll find out over the next two weeks).

Christians are like soldiers in God's army (but we don't fight with guns!). It's so encouraging to think that there are millions of believers out there fighting for the gospel by **telling people about Jesus**.

Pray!

If you're a believer, thank God that you are one of His army, His special people. Ask Him to give you the courage to serve Him.

Intense in tents

**Numbers
1 v 47-54**

There were 13
tribes of Israel
(well, two of
them were half
tribes).

But yesterday
we read that
only 12 tribes
were counted
for serving in the
army.

What about the
13th tribe?

Read Numbers 1 v 47-49

The tribe of Levi (the Levites) were
not counted, because they wouldn't
be doing any fighting (lucky them!).

Read verses 50-54

What was their special job? (v50)

The Levites were

in charge of the

t̲a̲b̲e̲r̲n̲a̲c̲l̲e̲

Tabernacle

A special, huge tent, where God
was present among His people. It
reminded the Israelites that God was
with them all the time.

Covenant law

Two big stones on which God had
written the Ten Commandments.
They were kept in a special box (the
ark of the covenant) inside the tent.

The Israelites were living in tents.
At the centre of their camp was the
tabernacle tent, which the Levites
looked after. They were responsible
for dismantling it, and setting it
up again, as they moved. Only
the Levites were allowed in the
tabernacle.

*What would happen to anyone else
who wandered into God's presence
in the tabernacle (v 51)?*

p̲u̲t̲ ̲t̲o̲ ̲d̲e̲a̲t̲h̲

Action!

How can you show God more
respect in your prayers, at school
and with other people?

T̲h̲a̲n̲k̲ ̲h̲i̲m̲

S̲h̲o̲w̲ ̲h̲i̲s̲ ̲l̲o̲v̲e̲ ̲t̲h̲r̲o̲u̲g̲h̲

m̲y̲ ̲a̲c̲t̲i̲o̲n̲s̲

WEIRD WORDS

Census
A count of the
population

Standard
Special flag

Wrath
God's anger and
punishment

Pray!

God is so awesome and powerful,
we shouldn't treat Him casually.
He's the boss of our lives. We
should show Him great respect.
Tell Him how totally awesome
you think He is now!

Numbers chapter 2 describes how the camp was set up. Read it if you like!

God's swap

Numbers 3

Remember the Levites from yesterday? They're going to be part of the swap! **Numbers 3 v 1-10** tells us about Aaron's family who were priests. God chose the Levites to be special helpers to the priests. And that's not all...

Read Numbers 3 v 11-13

How many Levites were there?

22,000

How many firstborn males were there?

22,273

How many more firstborn males than Levites?

273

Do you swap things with friends?

Yes

Today we'll read about a swap that God made.

History Snippet

When God rescued the Israelites from Egypt, He sent ten plagues on the Egyptians. In the final plague, the eldest son (the firstborn) in each family died. But God saved the lives of the eldest Israelite sons. They then belonged to God in a special way.

But now God said to Moses...

I have taken the
L e v i t e s instead of the
f i r s t b o r n

So now Moses has some more counting to do! (You can read all the details in verses 14-38.)

Not enough Levites to swap! For the left-over firstborn, the people had to pay God to buy them back (redeem them) from Him.

How many silver shekels for each firstborn?

5

How many shekels altogether?

1,365

Wow!

But what's that got to do with us? Well, God has REDEEMED us. By dying on the cross, Jesus PAID THE PRICE for our sins. If we've trusted Him to forgive us, we now BELONG to God!

Now read verses 39-51

Use these numbers to answer the questions below.

5

273

1,365

22,000

22,273

Pray!

Spend time thanking God for buying back His people. Thank Him that Christians belong to Him! They are His people!

WEIRD WORDS

Offspring
Children

Clans
Families

Livestock
Animals

Redeem
Buy back

Sanctuary shekel
About 58 grams

Exceeded
Were more than

Keep it clean!

Numbers 5 v 1-4

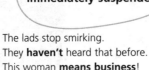
...and there will be no swearing in this school...

The lads at the back can't help smirking. They've heard that one before.

...and anyone using bad language will be immediately suspended.

It's school assembly, and the head teacher is boring everyone with the usual kind of lecture...

The lads stop smirking. They **haven't** heard that before. This woman **means business**!

It's not much use just saying something. People need to show that you **mean business**. God had a serious message to get over to the Israelites. **He knew that words on their own wouldn't sink in.**

WEIRD WORDS

Defiling skin disease
A nasty disease that made people unclean before God

Discharge
Icky stuff oozing from the body

Ceremonially unclean
Not clean enough to be near God

Read Numbers 5 v 1-4

God was living with His people. They had to be **clean** enough to be near God and to worship Him. The way God handled this uncleanness is a **picture** to us of something else...

Fill in the missing vowels (aeiou) to reveal what God was saying.

N <u>O</u> uncl <u>e</u> <u>a</u> n <u>e</u> ss
wh <u>e</u> re I l <u>i</u> ve

Disease was a picture of sin.

God has nothing against people with diseases; He loves them just as much. He was showing everyone how much He hates **sin**.

S <u>e</u> nd th <u>e</u> m aw <u>a</u> y
fr <u>o</u> m the c <u>o</u> mp

God didn't just **say** that He hates uncleanness. He meant business! And He wants His people to be **clean from sin**.

Pray!

Write down any sin you can't seem to get rid of.

Violence

Anger

Gossip

Ask God to help you turn away from this sin. It won't be easy and it may take a long time, but God can help you fight it!

**Verses 5-31 show how sin was dealt with.
Some of it sounds harsh but that's how seriously God takes sin.**

Nazirite angle

Numbers 6 v 1-21

We've discovered how the Levites served God in a special way by looking after the tabernacle.

But other people served God in a special way too.

Read Numbers 6 v 1-8

A Nazirite was someone who wanted to show their devotion to God in a special way. (Verses 9-21 describe other things Nazirites did — it was a hard, devoted life.)

Unjumble the anagrams to reveal what Nazirites promised.

I promise not to...

1. d r i n k   a n y
   k r i n d   n a y

   w i n e (v3)
   i n e w

2. c u t   m y
   u t c   y m

   h a i r (v5)
   r i h a

3. t o u c h   a
   c u t h o

   d e a d   b o d y (v6)
   e d d a   d o y b

Anyone could become a Nazirite. Anyone who really wanted to be separate from ordinary things and devote their lives to serving God. They tried very hard not to be contaminated by any sin.

These people were really **serious** about following God.

Think!

Are you serious about living for God? If you are, you might want to give up some things so that you can serve Jesus without getting distracted.

Action!

Is there anything you can give up or cut down on to help you serve God better? (Watch less TV? Stop swearing?)

Stop gossiping

Stop being angry + violent

Nazirites usually made these vows for just a **short time**. Christians are committed to obeying God and following Jesus their **whole lives**.

Pray!

Ask God to help you give up those things that get in the way of you living for Him.

Bless you!

**Numbers
6 v 22-27**

God loves His
people.

And today He
has an amazing
message for
them.

Let's check it out.

Read Numbers 6 v 22-27

This was God's great blessing for His
people. He told Moses exactly what
Aaron and the priests were to say.

*Let's find out what it meant. Use
the wordsearch to fill in the gaps.*

K	O	R	G	Z	A	N	B
E	L	Q	R	F	V	T	L
E	H	X	A	L	F	J	E
P	E	A	C	E	X	C	S
H	G	B	I	N	A	B	S
A	R	D	O	F	O	P	O
Z	G	T	U	R	N	C	K
S	C	D	S	H	I	N	E

The Lord b _l e s s_ you...

Blessings are good things that
God gives to His people. The best
blessing of all is being a friend of
God!

...and k _e e p_ you...

God will protect and look after His
people. He will always be with them
— they will be His special people
who belong to Him.

**...the Lord make His face
s _h i n e_ on you...**

God is always with His people. He
takes pleasure in them, accepts
them and treats them brilliantly!

**...and be g _r a c i o u s_
to you...**

God forgives the wrongs of people
who turn to Him even though they
don't deserve it.

**...and the Lord t _u r n_
His f _a c e_ towards you...**

God pays attention to His people.
He doesn't ignore them or make
them fend for themselves.

...and give you p _e a c e_

God looks after His people. He gives
them great peace. Ultimately, that
means living with Him for eternity.

Wow!

This brilliant blessing is true for all
of God's people (Christians)! Read
through it again... twice!

Pray!

Thank God that He loves and
cares for His people. sooo much.
Pick one or two sentences from
the blessing and spend time
thanking God for those great
truths.

Giving good gifts to God

1

Numbers 7

WEIRD WORDS

Tabernacle/ Tent of Meeting
Where God was present

Anointed and consecrated
Made pure and ready for God

Altar
Where gifts to God were put

Incense
Powder burned to make a sweet smell

Burnt offering
Cooked meat given to God

Atonement cover
The top of the ark

Ark of the Covenant Law
See end of the page

The Israelites had brought loads of gold and silver out of Egypt (see Exodus 12 v 35-36). God now told them what to do with it.

Read Numbers 7 v 1-6

Yesterday we read how God promised to **bless** His people. Now the people thanked and praised God by **giving** Him some of their treasures. First they gave carts and oxen to carry parts of the tabernacle. Then they gave valuable plates and dishes to be used in worshipping God.

Read verses 84-88 for a description of them.

It was a great time of devotion to God, lasting 12 days. This long chapter describes how each tribe brought their offerings to God.

Think!

The exact amount of what we give to God isn't so important. God cares about how generous and unselfish we are, and also HOW we give to Him.

Complete what Paul says in
2 Corinthians 9 v 7

God loves _____

_____

Action!

What can you give to God as a sign of your love for Him?

Pocket money? More time?

_____

_____

_____

Read verse 89

Do you remember the **ark**?

No, not Noah's ark! This ark was a special box which had the Ten Commandments in it (see the picture, top left). It was a big reminder that God was with His people. Moses heard God's voice coming from between the cherubim (angelic statues) on the top of the ark. God Himself spoke to Moses!

Pray!

God still speaks to His people today! We can read what God has to say to us in the Bible. Thank God that He is still with His people and that He speaks to us.

Sin solution

**Numbers
8 v 5-14**

*Let's discover
more about the
Levites and what
they got up to...*

God had chosen men from the tribe
of Levi to look after the tabernacle
— the special tent where God was
present. Let's check out some of the
things they had to do.

Read Numbers 8 v 5-14

*To show what the Levites had to do,
fill in the missing first letters.*

**1. Be __prinkled with __ater
and __have their whole
__odies and __ash their
__lothes (v7).**

To serve in God's special tent, in
God's presence, they had to be pure
and clean.

**2. The __sraelites were to lay
their __ands on the
__evites (v10).**

They put their hands on the heads
of the Levites to show that the
Levites were set apart to serve God
in this special way.

**3. They had to make
a __rain offering (v8),
a __in offering (v8),
and a __ave offering (v11)
to the Lord.**

Giving these gifts to God showed
their love and devotion to Him. The
most important one was the **sin
offering.**

When they sinned against God, an
animal was sacrificed so that the
Levite didn't have to be punished.

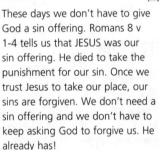

Wow!

These days we don't have to give
God a sin offering. Romans 8 v
1-4 tells us that JESUS was our
sin offering. He died to take the
punishment for our sin. Once we
trust Jesus to take our place, our
sins are forgiven. We don't need a
sin offering and we don't have to
keep asking God to forgive us. He
already has!

Pray!

Thank God for sending His Son
Jesus to be a sin offering for us.

For a free e-booklet on
why Jesus died, email
discover@thegoodbook.co.uk
or check out
www.thegoodbook.co.uk/contact-us
to find our UK mailing address.

WEIRD WORDS

**Ceremonially
unclean**
Clean enough to
be near God. It was
a picture to show
them how holy
God is!

Grain offering
Corn offered to
God as a gift

Wave offering
A gift of food,
waved in the air!

Atonement
Being forgiven and
having everything
put right with God

Passover party

**Numbers
9 v 1-14**

*It's time for a
celebration!*

*And EVERYONE
must join in!*

All of today's missing words are in
the word pool.

> away   celebrate   clean
> dead   failed
> fourteenth   Israelites
> journey   Moses   people
> Passover   twilight
> unclean

Read Numbers 9 v 1-5

The Lord said to M_____
(v1) "Make the Israelites
celebrate P_____ (v2)
at t_____ on the
f_____ day of
this month" (v3).

A year earlier the Israelites had put
lamb's blood on their doorposts to
escape the punishment God gave
the Egyptians. So every year they
had a **Passover** feast to remember
God **passing over** their houses and
only punishing the Egyptians.

Read verses 6-12

Some people couldn't
c_____ Passover
because they had touched
a d_____ body and so
were u_____ (v6).
God said these unclean
people and those a_____
on a j_____ could still
celebrate Passover (v10).

God wanted everyone to remember
what He had done for them.

Read verses 13-14

If anyone is c_____ and
f_____ to celebrate
Passover then they'd be cut
off from God's p_____
(v13). Foreigners living with
the I_____ could
celebrate Passover too (v14).

Anyone who didn't take part
would no longer be part of God's
people. God takes disobedience very
seriously.

Think!

Have you trusted in Jesus'
death to rescue you from the
punishment you deserve? If so,
then one day God will come to
judge everyone, but He will PASS
OVER you because Jesus died
instead of you!

Clouded judgment

We keep a close watch on the weather. It might make a difference to our plans for the day. If it's raining, there's not much chance of a barbecue!

The Israelites had a really good reason for keeping a very close watch on one particular cloud.

Read Numbers 9 v 15-23

The cloud was a sign that God was there with the Israelites.

If the cloud lifted from above the tent, what must they do?

But if it settled over the tent, they must...

Do you ever wake up and immediately pull open the curtains to see what the weather's like?

Go on, take a look right now...

Describe the weather outside in one word.

God was using the cloud to tell His people exactly when to move on and when to stay put.

Did they obey God's instructions?

YES/NO _____

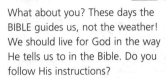

Think!

What about you? These days the BIBLE guides us, not the weather! We should live for God in the way He tells us to in the Bible. Do you follow His instructions?

If we follow God's commands, there's a great promise for us!

*Find it by taking **every 2nd letter**, starting with the T at the top.*

Isaiah 58 v 11

Pray!

What have you learned from God today?

_____

_____

_____

Ask God to help you put it into practice this week.

Attention!

**Numbers
10 v 1-10**

*Circle all the
things on the
right that are
used to grab your
attention.*

alarm clock   doorbell

rubber duck   phone

ambulance siren   feather

fire alarm   koala bear

car horn   ping pong ball

cheesecake   trumpet

*Which one do you think was used to
call the Israelites?*

Read Numbers 10 v 1-10

*Using the wordsearch, find the
five different occasions when the
Israelites needed to be alerted.*

K	H	S	J	E	Z	L	R	V
D	A	O	X	A	D	E	G	N
F	E	S	T	I	V	A	L	S
K	B	U	F	L	B	D	Q	C
Y	J	O	U	R	N	E	Y	A
T	C	L	P	F	J	R	E	M
E	L	T	T	A	B	S	C	P
C	O	Z	R	F	S	A	X	L

WEIRD WORDS

Ordinance
Law

Oppressing
Treating cruelly

Rejoicing
Overflowing with joy
and happiness

**New Moon
feasts**
Celebrations that
happened every
month to praise God

1. **Gathering everyone in the**
   c_____ (v2)
2. **Gathering the**
   l_____ (v4)
3. **Starting on a j_____**
4. **Going into**
   b_____ (v9)
5. **Special f_____**
   (v10)

Sometimes it was to gather them
to hear what God wanted to say
to them. At other times it was to
prepare them for action! There were
different trumpet signals so the
people always knew what they had
to do. But they always knew that
it was **God** who was calling their
attention.

Think!

God is calling for our attention
too! It's as though He is blowing a
trumpet to make us notice. Do you
take any notice of God, or do you
ignore Him?

Action!

Don't ignore God; do what He
says! Look up some of God's
instructions in the Bible.

• Acts 3 v 19
• Matthew 22 v 37
• Ephesians 4 v 26

Ask God to help you follow Him
when He calls and to obey His
instructions.

Get up and go

**Numbers
10 v 11-28**

Ever feel like you don't know what you're doing?

There was no chance of that for the Israelites!

WEIRD WORDS

Divisions
Groups

Standard
Banner

Holy things
See Numbers 3 v 31

Almost a year ago they had camped at Mount Sinai. Ever since, God had been giving them clear instructions for exactly how they should live.

Find Exodus 19 v 1. How many pages in your Bible from there to Numbers chapter 10?

All of that describes what God taught the Israelites at Mount Sinai! So they knew EXACTLY what God wanted them to do.

But now it was time to move!

Read Numbers 10 v 11-13

At last! Finally they were on their way to the land God had promised them (called Canaan).

Quickly read verses 14-28

They set off 3 tribes at a time, under their section leader. The Levites (Gershonites, Merarites and Kohathites) carried the different parts of the tabernacle.

Number the boxes 1-6 to show the order in which they set off.

Dan (3 tribes)	◯
Merarites & Gershonites	◯
Ephraim (3 tribes)	◯
Judah (3 tribes)	**1**
Kohathites	◯
Reuben (3 tribes)	◯

There was no confusion because they followed the instructions God had given them.

Think!

Look up the verses from yesterday's action box.

Are you following God's instructions? Which one do you need to work hardest on?

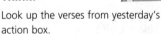

Pray!

Thank God that He gives us so much help in living His way. Ask Him to help you remember what He teaches you in the Bible, so that you live for Him more and more.

Land of Hobab's glory

Numbers
10 v 29-36

The Israelites are on the move.

They're going to Canaan, the land God promised to give them.

WEIRD WORDS

Midianite
From Midian, where Moses used to live and where he met his wife

Ark of the Covenant
See day 7

Foes
Enemies

Countless
Too many to count!

Which of these would you invite your friends along to?

Food at your house ☐

Football match ☐

Day at the beach ☐

Christian meeting ☐

The last one could be a bit embarrassing. But we care about our friends and want them to hear God's good news for them, don't we?

Moses cared about Hobab, his brother-in-law.

Read Numbers 10 v 29

Hobab wasn't an Israelite. But Moses really wanted him to share in the good things God had promised His people. If only Hobab would go with them and follow the Lord, he would be much better off.

Maybe you're afraid of what your friends might say? Read on to find out what Hobab said…

Read verses 30-32

Hobab wasn't rude, but his answer showed that he preferred his **own lifestyle** to following God.

We need to follow Moses' example. He couldn't bear the thought of Hobab rejecting God, so he tried again. Maybe he'd be able to persuade Hobab to change his mind…

> **Judges 1 v 16 suggests that Hobab gave in and his family lived with the Israelites!**

It would have been useful to have Hobab's help, but they had someone far better helping them.

Read verses 33-36

The Lord
…would find them places to camp!

The Lord
…would be looking after them!

Pray!

Thank God that He's with His people, guiding them through life. And ask God to help you tell your friends about Him and not give up when they turn you down.

Mind your mannas

Numbers
11 v 1-17

Read Numbers 11 v 1-9

The Israelites were ungrateful for all the great things God had done for them, like rescuing them from Egypt and feeding them with manna from heaven. They complained against God and Moses. It was more than Moses could take...

Read verses 10-15

Moses was saying to God...

Do you think God was angry with Moses?

YES/NO _____

WEIRD WORDS

Hardships
Tough times

Consumed
Burned down

Rabble
Non-Israelites who complained against God

Manna
Bread-like stuff that God rained down from heaven to feed them

Resin
Stuff like myrrh that comes from trees

Mortar
Bowl

Burden
Difficult thing

Conceive
Make them exist

What have I done
wrong for all this to
happen to me?

They're not my
own children. So why
should I have to look after
them all?

I can't give them
what they want!

I can't cope! Put me
to death rather than make
me carry on like this!

Use the letters with numbers above them to fill the spaces.

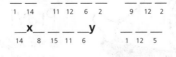

Read verses 16-17

Now decode what happened.

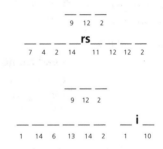

Nice one! God gave Moses **70 men** to help lead the Israelites!

Prayer action!

When you feel (like Moses) that everything is too much for you... TELL GOD HOW YOU FEEL. You know you shouldn't feel like you do, SO TELL GOD THAT TOO! He will understand. He will help you.

Meat to please you

Numbers
11 v 18-23

Do you ever whine?

If you complain long enough and LOUD enough, you might get your own way.

It's a bad habit to get into.

But did you know that God sometimes lets people have their own way?

The ungrateful Israelites have forgotten all the brilliant things God has done for them.

Like rescuing them from Egypt and feeding them.

They're complaining about not having enough meat to eat. They are rejecting God's way of living.

So God will give the Israelites just what they want. But so much of it that it will be coming out of their nostrils!

Read Numbers 11 v 18-20

God would punish them for rejecting Him and wanting their own way.

Wow!

If God lets you have your own way, you may regret complaining! God knows what's best for us much more than we do!

Read verses 21-22

Moses couldn't work out where all this meat would come from.

Moses seems to have forgotten that God had been miraculously raining bread on them for a year! And at the beginning, God had even given them enough meat to feed everyone.

Read God's reply in verse 23

God is saying that He is incredibly powerful. Does Moses think this would be too hard for God?

Is anything too hard for God?

YES/NO _____

Find Isaiah 59 v 1, write it out and learn it!

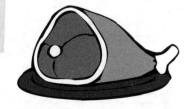

Pray!

Thank God that nothing is impossible for Him!

Team Spirit

Numbers
11 v 24-30

(Draw your own picture please. I couldn't think of what to put here!)

The Holy Spirit is God.

God gives His Spirit to live in the lives of all believers.

The Holy Spirit helps Christians live for God.

Read Galatians 5 v 22-23

and fill in the missing vowels.

The Holy Spirit helps

Christians to have...

l__ve   j__y   p__ __ce

f__rb__ __r__nc__

k__ndn__ss

g__ __dn__ss

f__ __thf__ln__ss

g__ntlen__ss

s__lf-c__ntr__l

Moses had God's Holy Spirit. Remember how God promised to give Moses 70 men to help him lead the Israelites (see Discover two days ago)?

Read Numbers 11 v 24-25

They needed the Holy Spirit to help them serve God.

When the Spirit

rested on them they

_____

Does that make you think of predictions about the future?

Prophesying in the Bible wasn't usually like that. Sometimes prophets would say important things about the future. But often it was more like preaching — telling people God's message.

Two of the seventy men were not prophesying in the same place as the others. So Joshua wanted to stop them. Moses didn't agree.

Read verses 26-30

> **I wish that all God's people had the Holy Spirit!**

Wow!

When Jesus went back to heaven, He gave His Spirit to live in the lives of **all** Christians!

Pray!

Thank God for His amazing gift of His Holy Spirit to help us live for Him. Look back at the list from Galatians (top left of the page). Ask God's Spirit to help you show these qualities in your life.

WEIRD WORDS

Forbearance
Patience

Elders
Leaders

Quails and wails

**Numbers
11 v 31-35**

God has given
the Israelites food
(manna) in an
amazing way. But
they've rejected
it!

*Instead, they are
demanding to eat
meat.*

*How cheeky is
that?!*

*Have you ever walked through a
snow drift? What's the deepest
snow you've ever been in?*

*Draw a line between the boy and
the **snow-o-meter** to show us.*

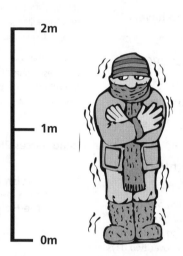

— 2m

— 1m

— 0m

Read verses 33-35

Bad news for the greedy Israelites.
The food they had wanted so
badly came with a deadly disease
from God.

**God punished them for
rejecting Him and living only for
themselves.**

Think!

What things are sometimes more
important to you than serving God?

_____

_____

_____

Imagine snow right up to your chest.
That's how much **meat** God sent
the Israelites! Almost a metre deep
in quail for miles around.

Quail
Birds like small
pheasants

Two cubits
About 1 metre

Ten homers
1000kg — that's
heavy!

Consumed
Eaten

Read Numbers 11 v 31-32

This was just what they'd been
wanting. Greedily they collected
piles and piles of the birds until
there were quails everywhere!

Think & pray!

Are you ever greedy like that?
Maybe not greedy for food — it
might be other things. Say sorry
to God and ask Him to help you
become less greedy.

Pray!

If you mean it, tell God that
you want to put Him FIRST. Ask
Him to help you turn away from
selfishness, greed and other
wrong things you do.

Jesus: The end?

**John
18 v 1-6**

*No time to waste!
We're jumping
into John's book
about Jesus' life.*

*We come in at a
crucial point, so
you need to be
prepared.*

*That means
prayer!*

WEIRD WORDS

Detachment
Group of soldiers

**Chief priests
and Pharisees**
Religious leaders
who wanted Jesus
dead. They sent
men *(officials)* to
arrest Him.

Pray!

Ask God to help you understand,
learn from and be excited by
what you read about Jesus over
the next couple of weeks.

Now read John 18 v 1-3

Judas had spent three years with
Jesus. He had travelled with Jesus,
seen Jesus do miraculous things,
and heard Jesus speak God's words!
But now he betrayed Jesus and led a
group of soldiers to arrest Him.

Read verses 4-6

*Verse 4 tells us something awesome
about Jesus. Cross out all the Bs, Qs
and Xs to find it.*

**JEBQQSUSKNEXWEVQBERY
THIXNGBTHXBATWXOUQLD
QBHAPQXPQENXXXTOHIBM**

J_ _ _ _   _ _ _ _

_ _ _ _ _ _ _ _ _ _ _

_ _ _ _   _ _ _ _ _

_ _ _ _ _ _

_ _   _ _ _ _

Wow!

Jesus knew that His friend Judas
would betray Him. And that He
would be arrested and killed. But
He also knew His Father, God, had
sent Him to earth just so He'd go
through these terrible events. It was
the only way that He could rescue
people from sin.

But Jesus wasn't helpless!

Read verse 6 again

The soldiers were overwhelmed just
being near Jesus, God's Son!

**JEBQQSBUSWBXBASIQQ
XNCOBBNXTQRBQXOLQ**

J_ _ _ _   _ _ _ _

_ _   _ _ _ _ _ _ _

Wow!

Jesus is God's Son! He could have
stopped the guards from arresting
Him. But He let it happen because
He knew it was all part of God's
great rescue plan.

The story continues tomorrow...

Time for arrest

John
18 v 7-14

Jesus is about to be arrested.

Today we'll spot three amazing things about Jesus' reaction to this scary situation.

WEIRD WORDS

Drink the cup
Obey God by dying

Bound him
Tied him up

Annas
He used to be High Priest (the most important Jewish leader) and was still very powerful

1. Care

Read John 18 v 7-9

Even at this tricky time, Jesus' first thoughts were not for Himself but for the safety of His friends!

Jesus was keeping His promise to protect His disciples (check out John 6 v 39).

Think & pray!

How do YOU measure up to Jesus' standard? Is your first instinct to look after yourself?

Or do you care enough for your friends to put them first?

PRAY that God will help you to care more for others.

2. Peace

Read verses 10-11

Jesus told Peter that violence wasn't the answer. Fill in Jesus' words to Peter from Matthew 26 v 52.

All who _____
the _____ will _____
by the _____.

Think & pray!

"I HATE YOU. YOU'RE SO ANNOYING AND BORING!"

How would you react if someone shouted that at you? Hit him? Insult him back?

Or follow Jesus' example?

PRAY for one person who treats you unfairly, that you'll be calmer with them.

3. Determination

Read verses 11-14

Even though Jesus didn't deserve to be arrested, He told Peter not to defend Him.

Shall I not
d_____ the c_____
which the F_____
has given me (v11)?

Think & pray!

That means: "Don't stop me from being arrested. It's all part of God's great plan." So Jesus let Himself be arrested.

PRAY — thank Jesus that He was prepared to go through such terrible things to obey His Father and rescue us.

Peter's not perfect

John
18 v 15-18

The disciples had run away when Jesus was arrested, but Peter wanted to stick close to his friend and master.

He managed to get himself into the high priest's courtyard, near where Jesus had been taken.

It was a dangerous move.

What would happen next?

Read John 18 v 15-17

Then fill in the speech bubbles on the right.

Read verse 18

First, Peter was caught off-guard by the slave girl and he denied knowing Jesus. Then he hung around the fire with the servants so no one suspected him.

Yesterday we read how Peter was prepared to fight for Jesus. Now he won't even own up to knowing Jesus!

Are you a Christian?

You don't got to church, do you???

Think!

How do you answer questions like that? Are you honest or too scared to own up?

_____

_____

_____

Read 1 Peter 3 v 15

Peter wrote that later on!
Cross out the wrong words.

Sometimes/Always/Never be prepared to give an answer/excuse to everyone/ nice people/no one who asks you to give the reason for the hype/hoop/hope that you have.

That means Christians should stand up for Jesus. And be ready to tell people about Him.

Pray!

Ask God to give you the courage to admit to knowing Jesus.

For a free fact sheet called *Telling Your Friends About Jesus,* email discover@thegoodbook.co.uk or check out www.thegoodbook.co.uk/contact-us to find our UK mailing address.

Trial and error

John
18 v 19-24

While Peter was warming his hands in front of the fire outside the high priest's house, Jesus was on trial inside.

But this was no ordinary court...

Read John 18 v 19

What two things did the high priest ask Jesus about? Go back one letter to find out (B=A, C=B).

_ _ _ _ _ _ _ _ _
E J T D J Q M F T

and _ _ _ _ _ _ _ _
U F B D I J O H

He probably wanted to know if Jesus had loads of disciples (followers) who would stand up for Him against the Jewish leaders. And he also wanted to know exactly what Jesus had been teaching.

That doesn't sound too unreasonable, does it?

But there were at least **three things missing** from this trial...

1. _ _ _ _ _ _ _
D I B S H F T

Read verse 20

Jesus had done nothing wrong. They had no charges against Him.

2. _ _ _ _ _ _ _ _ _
X J U O F T T F T

Read verse 21

Loads of people could have spoken up for Jesus, but didn't get the chance. And no one had any evidence against Him!

3. _ _ _ _ _ _ _ _
G B J S O F T T

Read verses 22-24

Despite having no evidence against Jesus, they wouldn't release Him. Instead, they attacked Him and sent Him to Caiaphas for another unfair trial.

Jesus was unfairly treated, tied up, hit and, later, far worse. Yet He was prepared to go through all of this to obey His Father and die for people who want to have their sins forgiven. Awesome!

Pray!

Do you have anything you want to say to God? You might even want to write out a prayer to Him.

Stand up or let down?

John
18 v 25-27

Jesus is on trial even though He has committed no crime.

Meanwhile, outside...

Peter is still warming himself by the fire in the high priest's courtyard. He has already denied knowing Jesus once.

Read John 18 v 25-27

Peter had now lied ____ times (remember v17 too).

Now think back to Jesus' last meal with His disciples…

Read John 13 v 37-38
Everything happened exactly the way Jesus had said it would.

How do you think Peter felt when he heard the cockerel crow? Tick your answers.

| ashamed | embarrassed |

| not bothered | annoyed |

| OK | like a traitor |

It's easy to be critical of Peter for turning his back on Jesus, but try this **Honesty Test**.

HOW MANY TIMES HAVE YOU...	0	1	2	more
said that you did "nothing much" on Sunday?				
kept quiet while people made fun of Jesus?				
felt too embarrassed to tell friends you're a Christian?				
been too afraid to say you believe what the Bible says?				

Are you still as critical of Peter, or do you feel like him? It's tough sometimes, but we should always try to stand up for Jesus.

WEIRD WORDS

Disown
Pretend not to know someone

Pray!

Take a little longer to pray today. Say sorry to God for the times you've let Him down. Ask Him to give you the courage to stand up for Him.

Pilate scheme

**John
18 v 28-32**

The Jewish leaders held two trials to try and convict Jesus, but there was no evidence against Him. Yet they were determined to have Jesus killed, so they took Him to Pilate.

Read John 18 v 28-30

These Jewish leaders were very careful in keeping some laws. They wouldn't enter the home of a Gentile person like Pilate at Passover time. But they weren't so bothered about other laws...

Th__ S__n __f M__n
w__ll b__ d__l__v__r__d
__v__r t__ th__
ch____f pr____sts
__nd th__ t__ __ch__rs
__f th__ l__w. Th__y
w__ll c__nd__mn H__m
t__ d__ __th __nd w__ll
h__nd H__m __v__r
t__ th__ G__nt__l__s
t__ b__ cr__c__f____d
(Matthew 20 v 17-19

Like breaking all the rules about fair trials! And they didn't care that they were trying to send an innocent man to his death.

Incredibly, despite the Jewish leaders' evil plot, it was **Jesus'** plans that were actually starting to work out...

Read verses 31-32
Jesus had predicted all of this! It wouldn't be the Jews who actually killed Him.

Fill in the missing vowels (aeiou) to complete what Jesus had said.

The Jewish leaders were not allowed to sentence anyone to death. But Pilate was a Roman, and he had the power to order that Jesus be crucified.

This was exactly what Jesus had said would happen. It was somehow all part of God's perfect plan!

WEIRD WORDS

Governor
Local ruler called Pilate

Ceremonial uncleanness
During Passover time, a Jew wasn't allowed to enter the house of a Gentile (non-Jew). If he did, he wouldn't be pure enough to celebrate Passover.

Passover
Feast to remember the time when God rescued His people from slavery in Egypt.

Pray!

Thank God that even when things seem to be going badly, it's all part of His perfect plan.

Captured King

**John
18 v 33-40**

Pilate

The Jewish leaders have taken Jesus to Pilate, the Roman governor.

They want Pilate to sentence Jesus to death.

Read John 18 v 33-35

Unjumble the anagrams to reveal what Pilate asked Jesus.

Are you the _____
G K N I

of the _____ ?
W E J S

To the Jews, claiming to be "King of the Jews" meant claiming to be the _____
N O S

of _____ (John 19 v 7).
O G D

They refused to believe the truth: Jesus **is** God's Son!

For Pilate and the Romans, "King of the Jews" meant a dangerous _____
E L D E R A

who would fight them.

The Jewish leaders hoped that Governor Pilate would suspect Jesus of leading a rebellion against the Romans, and sentence Him to death.

Read verses 36-37

Jesus said that He wasn't that kind of king. He hadn't come to fight against the Romans.

He came to earth to tell people the truth.

Wow!

Here's the truth about Jesus Christ — He is the King of all God's people (Christians). He now rules as their King in heaven!

Read verses 38-40

Tragedy. These people didn't realise that Jesus was the King, who had come to rescue people from their sinful ways. Instead, they were desperate to kill Him.

Pray!

Ask God to help you understand who Jesus really is, and to live with Him as the King in charge of your life.

King of pain

**John
19 v 1-5**

Things were going from bad to worse for Jesus.

Pilate knew that Jesus was innocent, but he was too scared of the Jewish people to let Jesus go free.

Read John 19 v 1-5

Flogging wasn't just a few soft whacks. The whip had pieces of bone and lead in it, and it was thrashed over the victim's bare back until it almost killed him.

Wow!

Jesus, King of the Universe, was cruelly mocked. He had a painful crown of thorns forced onto His head. And He was viciously flogged to within an inch of His life.

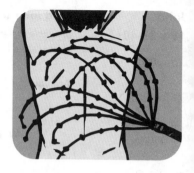

> **Can you ignore the amazing love of someone who'd go through all of that for you?!**

（hieroglyphic puzzle）

(1 Peter 4 v 13)

WEIRD WORDS

Flogged/ Scourged
Whipped many times

Hail!
Long live the King! They were mocking Jesus.

**If you haven't yet turned to Jesus, you can right now.
Say sorry for living your own way, and ask Him to forgive your sin.
He will!**

**If you're a Christian, how do you react when you have to suffer for Jesus (being teased etc)?
Decode the verse on the right!**

Pray!

If you really mean it, pray this prayer: "Dear God, thank you for sending your Son, Jesus. Please help me to understand why He went through all that pain and misery. Amen."

A	C	E	F	G	H	I	J	N	O	P	R	S	T	U	Y

Power point

CRUCIFY! CRUCIFY!

Read John 19 v 6-7

The Jewish leaders finally admitted the real reason why they wanted to see Jesus die (v7). *Find it by writing out the letters in* **white circles**, *in the same order.*

Read verses 8-10

What did Pilate say to Jesus? Scribble down the **grey circles**.

I _ _ _ _ _

_ _ _ _ _ _ _ _

_ _ _ _ _ _ _

_ _ _ _ _ _ _ _ _ _

_ _ _ **(v10)**

But what was Jesus' answer?

Read verse 11

Then use the **black circles**.

_ _ _ _ _ _ _ _

_ _ _ _ _ _ _ _

_ _ _ _ _ _ _

_ _ _ _ _ **(v11)**

The Jewish leaders want Pilate to sentence Jesus to death.

Pilate had Jesus cruelly flogged, but he's still refusing to send innocent Jesus to His death...

(Circle puzzle grid:)

H I P E O H A C
V W L A E P I O
E W E M R E I R
T D S T O G F O
B I R E E V E E
N Y T H T O E U
O O Y S O R U C
F R O R N U O C
M I O A F F B Y
O V G Y O E O D U

H_ _ _ _ _ _ _ _

_ _ _ _ _ _ _

_ _ _ _ _ _ _ _

They refused to believe that Jesus was God's Son.

God is in control of everything! Pilate only had power over Jesus because God let him have it. It was all part of **God's perfect plan!** Pilate didn't want to kill Jesus, but high priest Caiaphas did — so he was more guilty than Pilate (v11).

WEIRD WORDS

Crucify
Kill someone by nailing them to a wooden cross and then leaving them to die

Pray!

...for people you know who refuse to believe in Jesus. Ask God to open their eyes to the truth.

Pray!

Thank God that even when things seem to be going wrong, He's the one with the power. He's in control and His plans always work out!

Caesar's geezers

**John
19 v 12-16**

The pressure's on for Pilate.

He wants to let Jesus walk free, but he's far too scared of the Jewish leaders and their devious threats.

What will he do?

WEIRD WORDS

Caesar
Roman Emperor

Aramaic
Language spoken by Jewish people

Day of Preparation
Friday

Read John 19 v 12-16

*Then, if you're feeling clever, I'll challenge you to the **Multi-Choice Challenge**...*

1. Why did Pilate try to set Jesus free?

a) he was a kind and caring judge ☐

b) he knew Jesus was innocent ☐

c) he wanted to go home for his tea ☐

2. How did the Jewish leaders trap Pilate?

a) accused him of breaking the law ☐

b) threatened him with big pointy sticks ☐

c) threatened to accuse him of betraying Caesar ☐

3. Who did the Jews say was their king?

a) Caesar ☐

b) Jesus Christ ☐

c) Henry VIII ☐

4. So what did Pilate do?

a) let Jesus go free ☐

b) threw the Jewish leaders in prison ☐

c) handed Jesus over to be crucified ☐

Check your answers at the bottom of the page.

The Jewish leaders claimed to have "no king but Caesar" (v15).

Wrong! **Jesus was their King**, yet they refused to see it. So they turned down Jesus and turned their backs on God.

Think!

How about you? Surely you're not like these guys at all...

• When Jesus challenges you through the Bible, or makes you feel uncomfortable about your sin, do you push the thoughts away?

• Have you asked Jesus to be your King? Or do you keep pushing Him away?

Cross purpose

John
19 v 17-22

You might have read about Jesus' crucifixion many times.

And heard about it even more.

Well, God's still got amazing things to tell us about the death of His Son.

Pray!

Ask God to show you something awesome and new about His love today.

Read John 19 v 17-22

for the awful truth.

Now fill in the gaps from what you've just read.

Jesus' back and face were bleeding from the beating He'd had (v1-3). He must have been exhausted, yet He still had to c__ __ __y His own
1
c__ __ __s (v17). He had to
2
s__ __fer the __eath of a
10 7   8
crimina__, along with t__o
9   3
thie__es (v18).
4
A sign stated that His only crime was being K__ __ __ __
6
of the __ __ __ __.
5

```
IESVS·NAZARENVS·
REX·IVDÆORVM
ιησους ο ναζωραιος ο
βασιλευς των ιουδαιων
ישוע הנצרי ומלך היהודים
```

It sounds terrible, yet Jesus went through this incredible pain and shame **for sinners like us!**

Now complete the sentence below, using the letters you filled in earlier.

It showed His

__ __ __ __ __ __ __ __
3 2 6 8 5 1 7 10 9

__ __ __ __
9 2 4 5

Pray!

It's up to you today. No help. After seeing what Jesus went through, what do you want to say to Him?

_____

_____

_____

_____

_____

_____

WEIRD WORDS

Aramaic
A Jewish language

Latin
Official language of the Romans

Greek
Language that many people spoke

Dicing up clothes

John
19 v 23-27

Jesus is on the cross, dying.

But that didn't stop the soldiers taking His things...

WEIRD WORDS

Decide by lot/ cast lots
Throw dice to decide

Scripture
Old Testament

Disciple whom Jesus loved
John, whose book we're reading!

Read John 19 v 23-24

What an awful thing to do — taking the clothes of a dying man. Little did the soldiers know they were doing what was predicted in the Old Testament!

*Look it up in **Psalm 22 v 18** and fill in the gaps below.*

They_____

_____

_____

and_____

_____

_____

Wow!

King David wrote those words 1000 years before Jesus was crucified! They came true in every detail. God's Word, the Bible, is totally 100% reliable and true. We can trust it completely!

Read verses 25-27

Jesus was in agony — but that didn't stop Him caring for His mother and making sure she would be looked after.

Action!

How can you follow Jesus' example? Who can you show more love and care for? How will you do it?

_____

_____

_____

_____

_____

_____

God cares for, and looks after, all Christians. But don't take my word for it. Read what David wrote in **Psalm 23**.

You might even want to write it out and stick it on your wall.

Pray!

Thank God that He looks after His children, Christians. And ask His help in doing the stuff you wrote down under *Action!*

30 The end for Jesus?

**John
19 v 28-30**

Finally, Jesus' death, the most important event in world history, reached its climax.

WEIRD WORDS

Scripture
Old Testament

Fulfilled
Come true

Wine vinegar
Cheap alcoholic drink

Hyssop
Bushy plant

Gall
Probably a bitter, poisonous plant

For the free e-booklet *Why Did Jesus Die?* email discover@thegoodbook.co.uk or check out www.thegoodbook.co.uk/contact-us to find our UK mailing address.

Read John 19 v 28-30

What were Jesus' last words before He died (v30)?

_____

Hold on a moment...

WHAT WAS FINISHED???

Well, three things actually...

1. Old Testament prophecies

Scribble down Psalm 69 v 21

_____

_____

Now compare it with John **19 v 29**. The last prediction about Jesus' death had come true. It was time for Him to give up His life.

2. Jesus' suffering

The shame. The physical pain. The unfairness. And worst of all, the awfulness of God's anger against His people's sin. All of that was now over.

3. Jesus' work

Jesus had achieved the great purpose of His life.

On the cross, He took the punishment we deserve. So everyone who turns to Him can have their sin forgiven!

Don't even think of rejecting Jesus' gift of forgiveness!

The story of Jesus doesn't end there: More from John's story of Jesus in a couple of weeks...

Numbers: Off to Canaan

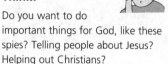

Numbers
13 v 1-3

Time to catch up with Moses and the Israelites.

God rescued them from slavery in Egypt and now He's leading them through the desert.

The Israelites have almost reached the land God has promised to give them — Canaan.

Read Numbers 13 v 1-3

It's spy time. Use the code to answer the questions.

Who was being sent out?

To do what?

Why was the land special?

Think!

Do you want to do important things for God, like these spies? Telling people about Jesus? Helping out Christians?

Notice that the spies (mentioned in v4-16) were already leaders. They had shown that they wanted to serve God by doing smaller jobs, before being trusted with bigger jobs like spying.

Don't wait to start serving God. Start with the opportunities you have right now. Why not try...

- **visiting elderly people you know**
- **odd jobs around church**
- **setting up a youth prayer meeting**
- **something else...**

Pick two things you could do.

1.

2.

WEIRD WORDS

Ancestral tribe
There were 12 Israelite tribes. Each one was made up of the descendants (family) of Joseph or one of his 11 brothers.

Pray!

Ask God to help you do the things you've written down. Make sure you do them this week! NO excuses!

A	B	D	E	F	G	H	I	L	M	N	O	P	R	S	T	X

I spy with my little...

**Numbers
13 v 17-21**

*The Israelites
are on the edge
of the land God
has promised to
give them.*

*They're sending
twelve spies to
check it out...*

> I spy, with my little eye,
> something beginning
> with C.

Cat?
Cow?

Chocolates?

Have you got any idea?

C_____

The answer is Canaan. Moses is
sending spies to check it out.

Read Numbers 13 v 17-21
*and fill in what they had to discover
about....*

God had already told the Israelites
something about the land they
would be living in. Check it out in
Exodus 3 v 8.

He wanted them to **check it out
for themselves**. It's like that for
people finding out about living for
God, becoming a Christian.

Think!
Have you checked out...

• how to become a Christian?

• the kind of life a Christian lives?

• the hard things you'll face?

• the amazing things God gives His
  people, both now, and in heaven?

WANT TO KNOW MORE ABOUT ONE
OF THOSE THINGS?

Tell us which one and we'll send
you a free fact sheet or some more
information. Email
discover@thegoodbook.co.uk
or check out
www.thegoodbook.co.uk/contact-us
to find our UK mailing address.

WEIRD WORDS

The Negev
A desert

Fortified
Protected by huge
walls

Fertile
Good for growing
crops

the people (v18)

the towns (v19)

the land (v20)

Pray!
Ask God to help you discover
more about living for Him.

Anakrophobia

Numbers 13 v 22-29

Twelve spies have gone into Canaan to check it out. Let's look at their reports...

Read Numbers 13 v 22-25

How long did they spend spying?

_____ days

Loads of time to check it out properly. They even had time for a large doggy bag! (v23)

Read verses 26-29

*What did the spies say about the land, the people and the cities? Each one was either **great** news or a big **problem**. Mark the correct answer for each one.*

The land
great ☐
problem ☐

The people
great ☐
problem ☐

The cities
great ☐
problem ☐

Defeating the people who were already living in the land wasn't going to be easy. But God had shown the Israelites that the land He'd promised them was worth waiting for.

Think!

Do you ever think living God's way is too hard? In the Bible, God shows us how great the future will be with Him.

It reminds us that the end result will be worth it.

Wow!

Christians can be God's friends now, and will live with Him for ever! Living God's way won't be easy.

It can be really tough at times. But it will be worth the hard work and the hassle.

Pray!

Talk to God about the things that make you consider giving up.

_____

_____

_____

_____

Ask Him to help you keep going and to show you that it's worth it.

For the free fact sheet *Facing Tough Times*, email discover@thegoodbook.co.uk or check out www.thegoodbook.co.uk/contact-us to find our UK mailing address.

WEIRD WORDS

The Negev
Desert area

Descendants of Anak
Very large people, like giants

Pomegranates
Red fruit with loads of seeds

Eshkol
Means cluster

Fortified
Well protected

The Jordan
Big river

Giants and grasshoppers

Numbers
13 v 30-33

The twelve spies have checked out Canaan.

But not all their reports say the same thing

Read Numbers 13 v 30-33

Fill in the two different reports.

Caleb

We should _____

_____

_____

_____

_____(v30)

Caleb trusted God and wanted to capture the land God had promised to give them.

The other spies

They are _____

than we are! (v31)

The spies were so scared, they even made the problems sound worse than they were.

The people are of great size. We seem like

g_____

compared to them (v33)

They were exaggerating the truth, to scare the people away from Canaan. The spies had forgotten God's promise to them. Look it up in **Exodus 3 v 17**. How cool is that promise?!

God had promised that He would give them the land. And He's **loads more powerful** than the people the spies saw, no matter how big they were.

Things may have looked bad, but only when they **forgot about God**. With Him on their side there was nothing to worry about!

Think!

The spies said they trusted God but their actions showed they didn't. What do your actions show about who you trust? Does the way you live show that you follow Jesus?

WEIRD WORDS

Devours
Eats and destroys, like a hungry wolf!

Nephilim
People of great size and strength (see Genesis 6 v 4)

Pray!

Say sorry to God for forgetting that He's in control. And for worrying about stuff too much. Ask Him to help you TRUST Him. And to put that trust into ACTION.

Somethin' stupid

**Numbers
14 v 1-4**

*Ever done something really stupid?
Like putting salt on your cornflakes?
Or forgetting where you live?*

In today's Bible bit, the Israelites are far more stupid than that.

Where did the Israelites say they should go (v4)?

_____

Most of the spies told lies that the land of Canaan was full of giants.

The Israelites became terrified.

Read Numbers 14 v 1-4

What did they wish had happened to them (v2)?

_____

_____

STUPID THING 3
They said they'd rather go back to Egypt!

They had been treated terribly in Egypt (Exodus 1 v 11-16). But God had rescued them from their horrible life there!

STUPID THING 1
They wished they were dead

Even though they had finally arrived at a land full of good things that God had promised to give them! (Check out Numbers 13 v 27)

The Israelites weren't just being stupid, they were **insulting God.** It was like saying...

> **I don't trust your plans. I don't believe your promises. I can do better on my own.**

WEIRD WORDS

Whole assembly
Everyone

Fall by the sword
Be killed by enemies

Plunder
Things taken from a defeated enemy

What did they think God would let happen (v3)?

_____

_____

STUPID THING 2
They thought God would let them all die

But He had promised to lead them to live in Canaan (Exodus 3 v 17).

Think!

Do you ever insult God by thinking you know better than Him? Ignoring God and doing things your way instead?

Pray!

Say sorry to God for the times you've done things your own way and ignored Him.

Rebel without a clue

**Numbers
14 v 5-10**

*The Israelites
are turning
against God
again.*

*They don't trust
Him and don't
believe His
promises.*

Read Numbers 14 v 5-8

Joshua and Caleb were disgusted.
They couldn't believe the way the
people were treating God.

*Cross out the Xs, Ys and Zs to
reveal what they did.*

YYXTZOXYZXRZYEYZ

ZXTHZXYEIZXRYCXLZY

OXTYXYHZYXZEYSXZZ

T_____

_____(v6)

This was their way of showing
sadness and regret.

*What were Joshua and Caleb's
reasons for going into Canaan?
Cross out the untrue bits.*

The land is...
exceedingly good/rubbish

There is...
no food/loads of good food
like milk and honey

God...
doesn't care/will lead us into
this land

Canaan had everything the Israelites
needed. And God had promised to
give Canaan to them! What was
their problem?

Read verse 9

*Cross out the Xs, Ys and Zs to find
Joshua and Caleb's warning.*

XYDOZNOXZTREYXY

BEZZZLAXYGAZYINSX

ZYTTHYELZZORXDY

D_____

_____

That goes for us too! We should be
living for God, not against Him.

Read verse 10

*Circle the word that describes the
reaction of the people.*

JOY   ANGER   REGRET

How do you react when your sin
is pointed out to you? Do you get
angry and sulky? Do you try to
cover it up? Or do you regret it,
admit it to God and tell Him how
sorry you are?

Enough's enough!

**Numbers
14 v 10-12**

*The Israelites are
turning against
God again.*

*But this time
God has had
enough of their
disobedience.*

Read Numbers 14 v 10-12

Is God being fair? Time to remind
ourselves of some of the things that
had happened since the Israelites
left Egypt...

1. At the Red Sea
(Exodus 14)

> Was it because there
> were no graves in Egypt
> that you brought us to
> the desert to die?

God rescued them from slavery in
Egypt. Yet immediately they were
doubting Him. Amazingly, God
parted the Red Sea to let them
escape.

2. In the Desert
(Exodus 16)

> You have brought us into
> the desert to starve us all
> to death!

So God gave them manna bread
and quail to eat.

3. And now... (Numbers 14)

> If only we had died in
> the desert!

But this time God said...

> **HOW MUCH LONGER
> WILL THEY REFUSE TO
> BELIEVE IN ME?!**

They had gone too far. It was time
for God to punish them (v12).

*Write out **Romans 6 v 23***

_____

_____

_____

_____

_____

It's the same for us. One day God
will punish everyone who refuses to
believe in Him and live His way. But
if we trust Jesus to forgive us, we
can live with God for ever!

WEIRD WORDS

Whole assembly
Everyone

Glory of the Lord
What God is actually
like

Tent of Meeting
The tabernacle, a
tent where God was
present

Contempt
Hatred and lack of
respect

Pray!

Thank God for His great patience.
Say sorry for the times you don't
trust Him. Ask Him to help you
stop disobeying Him.

Pleading heart

**Numbers
14 v 13-20**

The Israelites keep disobeying God.

So God has decided to destroy them and start again with just Moses and his family.

What do you reckon Moses thought about this?

Read Numbers 14 v 13-19

Moses was worried about what other nations would think of God if He punished His people like this.

What arguments did Moses use to plead with God? Use the wordsearch to fill in the blanks.

O	D	B	F	X	G	T	C
H	P	E	O	P	L	E	R
S	Z	S	R	A	K	B	Y
I	A	V	G	N	F	Q	L
N	A	T	I	O	N	S	A
S	L	O	V	I	N	G	N
P	E	J	E	C	G	O	D
Z	L	O	P	G	V	C	A

1. Egypt and the other n_____ would think that G_____ was not able to bring His p_____ into the l_____ (v13-16).

2. Moses knew the Lord was a l_____ God so He could still f_____ the people's s_____ (v19).

Moses asked God to be **loving** and **forgiving** towards the Israelites because he knew that God is both loving and forgiving.

So what happened?

Read verse 20

The Israelites deserved to be destroyed but God showed His love for them by forgiving them again!

WEIRD WORDS

Inhabitants
People who live there

Oath
Promise

Abounding
Full of it!

Rebellion
Turning against God

Pardoned
Forgiven

Pray!

Thank God for not changing His mind about saving His people. Now think of people you know who refuse to live God's way. Ask God to show His love to them so that they turn to Him for forgiveness.

Rough justice

**Numbers
14 v 20-30**

*Moses has
pleaded with
God not to wipe
out the Israelites,
even though they
keep turning
away from Him.*

God said He wouldn't destroy the
people even though they deserved
to die.

Read Numbers 14 v 20-30

> **Hold on, I thought
> God said that He was
> forgiving the people.
> Now He's saying most of
> them will die in the desert
> instead of going into
> Canaan. What's
> going on?**

*Add the vowels (aeiou) to see what
God said (verses 23-24).*

N__ __n__ wh__
r__j__ct__d m__ w__ll
s__ __ th__ l__nd.
C__l__b f__ll__ws m__,
so I w__ll br__ng h__m
__nt__ th__ l__nd.

Yesterday we saw that God is
merciful — forgiving people even
though they deserve to be punished.
Today we see another side of God's
character: **justice**.

Two important words

Mercy
To show someone kindness that
they don't deserve.

Justice
Making sure that sin is punished and
good is rewarded.

It's a bit like a coin. Both sides are
part of the same coin, you can't
have one without the other.

Because God is **merciful**, He didn't
destroy the Israelites and wipe them
out for ever. But because He is **just**
He had to punish their sin.

God's punishment would be for His
people to head back towards the
Red Sea and Egypt. Just what these
ungrateful people had wanted (look
back at v2).

*But two people would be allowed to
eventually live in the land God had
promised them. Who? (v30)*

C_____ & J_____

They were the two spies who had
told the truth and trusted God to
take them into Canaan.

Wow!

God punishes everyone who
disobeys Him. But if we trust in
Him like Joshua and Caleb did,
then He will forgive us. And we
will go to live in the perfect place
God has promised His people.

Meet the parents

Numbers 14 v 31-35

Are you still a little confused from yesterday's Bible bit?

How can God forgive the Israelites and yet still not let them enter the promised land?

WEIRD WORDS

Plunder
Things taken from a defeated enemy

Unfaithfulness
Turning away from living God's way

Read Numbers 14 v 31-35

What the Israelites deserved

To be struck down and destroyed by God (v12).

What the Israelites got

They would eventually die in the desert (v32). Their children would get to enjoy the promised land of Canaan (v31).

Write GOOD NEWS or BAD NEWS at the top of each box below.

> _____ **NEWS**
> for the grumbling grown ups. They were eventually going to die in the desert and not enter the promised land.

> _____ **NEWS**
> for the grumbling grown ups. God wouldn't immediately destroy them, as they deserved.

> _____ **NEWS**
> for the children. They would get to enjoy the fantastic land that God had promised.

> _____ **NEWS**
> for the children. Because of their parents' sins, they'd spend 40 years wandering in the desert before they got to Canaan.

Think!

The sins of the parents affected the children. Our sin affects the people around us. How does the wrong stuff you do affect other people?

Match the sins to the effects.

Sin	Effect on others
selfishness	hurt feelings
laziness	loss of trust
unkind words	extra work
lies	lose out

Pray!

Say sorry for particular times when your sins have had an effect on others. Ask God to help you to be more considerate of other people.

Poisonous people

**Numbers
14 v 36-38**

What would happen to the ten spies who lied about Canaan and got everyone grumbling against God?

Just one drop of poison in a glass of water ruins the whole drink.

Read Numbers 14 v 36-38

What does verse 37 say these spies had done?

They had spread a b_____

r_____ and lied about

what Canaan was like.

What was their punishment?

They d____d of a p_____

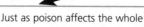

> They got the punishment they deserved.

> The words of just ten men **poisoned** the minds of all the Israelites, affecting millions of people.

> Just as poison affects the whole glass of water. Everyone started grumbling against God.

> Because of these spies, loads of people turned against God, so God had to punish them.

What sort of an influence do you have on the people around you?

| Do you stand up for God at school?
YES/NO | Or do you put people off as the spies did?
YES/NO |

God holds us responsible for the report we give others

For the free fact sheet *How To Tell Your Friends About Jesus*, email discover@thegoodbook.co.uk or check out www.thegoodbook.co.uk/contact-us to find our UK mailing address.

Pray!

Ask God to help you have a good influence on your friends and family, telling them about Jesus. Pray that the way you live would make them more interested in Christianity.

Too late to turn back

Numbers
14 v 39-45

God has just punished the ten spies who turned the Israelites against Him.

They got the death penalty they deserved.

Read Numbers 14 v 39-40
Did the Israelites do right or wrong at each stage?

They mourned bitterly (v39)
RIGHT/WRONG _____

"We have sinned" (v40)
RIGHT/WRONG _____

They decided to do what God had originally said (v40)
RIGHT/WRONG _____

The Israelites were **right** on the first two, but what about the third one? Let's find out...

You people are
_____ the Lord's command (v41) and
_____ away from the Lord (v43).
This will not
_____! (v41)
You will be
_____
by your enemies (v42).
You will _____ by the
_____ (v43).

It was too late! The people were finally obeying God's original command to go into Canaan.

But only because they didn't like His new instructions! They were still more interested in doing what sounded easiest than obeying God.

Read verses 44-45
Even after all this, the Israelites still insisted on doing what **they** thought was best instead of trusting God.

WEIRD WORDS

Mourned
Were hugely upset

Ark of the Lord's Covenant
Large wooden box that was a sign of God being with His people (see the picture at the top)

Read verses 41-43
How does Moses describe what they wanted to do? Use the word pool to fill in the gaps.

sword   succeed

turning   disobeying

fall   defeated

Think & pray!

What about you? Do you live to please God or to please yourself? Want to tell God about it right now? Ask Him to help you obey Him immediately.

Offer you can't refuse

**Numbers
15 v 22-29**

*It's time to make
a sacrifice...*

The Israelites rejected God's plan to
take them into Canaan to live there
and have it as their own country.
As punishment, a whole generation
would die in the desert. Their
children would get to live in Canaan
in the future.

Wow!

Even though these people kept
disobeying God, He would still
keep His promise to take them
into Canaan. God always keeps His
promises!

Verses 1-21 of chapter 15 mention
some of the laws the Israelites had
to keep if they wanted to live God's
way from now on.

Read Numbers 15 v 22-29

If anyone accidentally broke one
of God's laws, they had to make
special **offerings** (also called
sacrifices) to God. If they gave God
these offerings, God would **forgive**
their sin (v28).

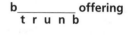

*Unjumble the anagrams to show the
different offerings mentioned in v24.*

b_____ offering
t r u n b

g_____ offering
a r g i n

d_____ offering
k r i n d

s_____ offering
i n s

These days we don't make offerings
to God when we've sinned. Here's
why...

Read Hebrews 10 v 8-10

Wow!

Jesus gave Himself as an offering to
God from us. He died on the cross
so that our sins can be forgiven.
Everyone who trusts in what Jesus
did for them by dying, has ALL their
sins forgiven by God!

Pray!

Spend time thanking Jesus for
dying on the cross so that people
can have their sins forgiven.
Thank Him for being the perfect
offering to God.

Tassel hassle

**Numbers
15 v 30-41**

Yesterday we discovered what the Israelites had to do if they sinned accidentally. But what if someone disobeyed God on purpose?

Read Numbers 15 v 30-31

If someone deliberately went against God's commands, they would be punished.

Read verses 32-36

It sounds harsh, doesn't it? But this man had disobeyed God deliberately. The Sabbath (Saturday) was a special day that God had given His people for rest. This man refused to obey God and so was punished.

Wow!

God takes sin very seriously. We need to remember how God feels about us disobeying Him before we choose to do wrong. Thankfully God has made it possible for us to have our sins forgiven (read yesterday's Discover page if you need a reminder).

Read verses 37-41

Fill in the missing vowels (aeiou).

They put t__ss__ls on the c__rn__r of their clothes (v38). The tassels reminded them to ob__y the c__mm__nds of the L__rd (v39). They wanted to obey God because He had rescued them from __gypt (v41).

Christians want to obey God because He has rescued them from sin. They want to live His way instead of disobeying Him.

To remind yourself to live God's way you could...

1. stitch a tassel on to your favourite clothes

2. make a poster with the 10 Commandments (Exodus 20 v 1-17) on it

3. write *LIVE GOD'S WAY* on stickers or notelets. Put them in 6 places you look most often (mirror, mobile phone, school bag, bedroom door etc)

Action!

What will you do to remind yourself to live God's way?

_____

_____

Ask God to help you do it!

Rotten rebellion

**Numbers
16 v 1-15**

WEIRD WORDS

Reubenites
People from the tribe of Reuben

Insolent
Disrespectful

Holy
Set apart to serve God

Censers
Containers in which incense was burned

Incense
Powder that was burnt to make a sweet smell

Levites
Tribe who served God in a special way

Tabernacle
Huge tent where God was present

Moses and Aaron were God's messengers to the Israelites.

But not everyone was happy with them. *Today's missing words are in the centre.*

Read Numbers 16v1-3

K_____, Dathan and A_____ rose up against Moses (v1). They had _____ men with them (v2). They didn't think M_____ and A_____ should tell them what to do (v3).

Read verses 4-11

Moses told Korah that the L_____ would show them who really was h_____ (v5). He said to the L_____: *"Isn't it enough that God has brought you n_____ Himself to do the work at the t_____? (v9). You have banded together against the Lord."*

Centre column: Aaron kill land Abiram Levites 250 Lord angry lord Dathan Moses near desert holy tabernacle honey Korah wronged

Read verses 12-15

D_____ and Abiram refused to go to Moses (v12). They moaned *"Isn't it enough that you brought us out of the l_____ of milk and h_____ to k_____ us in the d_____ (v13)? Now you want to l_____ it over us!" (v13).* Moses told God how a_____ he was, because he had not w_____ them at all (v15)!

Think!

Are you ever dissatisfied with what God has given you? Do you ever moan about the people who teach you about God?

And when people unfairly moan about you, do you turn nasty on them? Or, like Moses, do you turn to God for help?

Pray!

Say sorry to God for times you wrongly moaned about Him or someone who serves Him. Anything else bothering you that you need to tell God?

Eaten by the earth!

**Numbers
16 v 16-50**

*Korah, Dathan,
Abiram and 250
others refused
to listen to
God's servant
Moses.*

*God was going
to show them
who was really
on His side...*

WEIRD WORDS

Censer
Incense burner

Contempt
Hatred

Altar
Where offerings to
God were put

Atonement
Deal with their
sin so they'll be
forgiven

Wrath
Anger

Read Numbers 16 v 16-35

Cross out the wrong answers.

Moses, Aaron and their
2/25/250 enemies (v17) stood
outside the Tent of Meeting/
Measles with their incense
burners (v18). God was going
to destroy all the Israelites
for turning against Moses.
But Moses and Aaron fell
on their feet/fences/faces
and asked God not to kill
everyone (v22). The earth
opened up and swallowed/
spat out Kevin's/Korah's men
(v32). The Lord also sent
flies/fire/firemen to burn up
the 250 men who had turned
against Moses (v35). Now
everyone knew that Korah/
Moses was the one sent by
God (v28).

Read verses 36-40

The Lord told Eleanor/Eleazar
(Aaron's son) to hammer
all the incense burners
together and put them over
the ark/altar (v38). This was
to annoy/bully/remind the
Israelites to obey God (v40).

Think!
Look at the Action! box from two
days ago. Have you made yourself
reminders to live God's way yet?

Read verses 41-50

Amazingly, all the Israelites
still mumbled/grumbled
against Moses and Aaron
(v41)! God's glory appeared
in a star/cloud/clown
(v42) to put an end to the
disobedient people. Many
died of a cold/plague (v49)
but Moses/Dathan/Aaron
stopped many more from
dying (v48-49).

These people deserved to die for
turning against God again and
again. One day, God will punish
everyone who refuses to live His
way. But, like Aaron, we can do
something about it. We can tell
people about Jesus and pray for our
friends and family who aren't yet
living for God.

Pray!
Think of at least three people you
know who don't live God's way.
Now spend five minutes pleading
with God to rescue them so they
turn to Him and have their sins
forgiven.

Startling staff stuff

**Numbers
17 v 1-13**

Yesterday we read how God made the earth swallow up Korah and his family for turning against Moses. But that wasn't enough proof for the people, so He would show them one more time.

Read Numbers 17 v 1-9

The Israelites are grumbling against Moses and Aaron being the leaders of the Israelites.

What did Moses do with the staffs of the 12 tribe leaders (v2-4)?

What would happen to the staff of the man God chose to serve Him (v5)?

What happened to Aaron's staff (v8)?

That's a miracle! God gave the Israelites amazing proof that He had chosen **Aaron** to serve Him in a special way.

Read verses 10-13

What did they think would happen to them (v12)?

But God had done this amazing thing so that they'd finally stop complaining and He wouldn't have to punish them (v10). One day, God will punish everyone who refuses to obey Him. But He wants us to turn to Him instead.

Find Romans 5 v 8 and write it out here:

WEIRD WORDS

Staffs
Walking sticks

Ancestral tribes
Every Israelite was in one of 12 family tribes

Levi
Tribe chosen to serve God

Testimony/ Covenant law
10 Commandments

Rebellious
People going against God

Tabernacle
Special tent

Pray!

Thank God that He loves us so much and that He doesn't want to punish us. Thank Him for sending Jesus to rescue us from our sinful lives.

More from Numbers in a few weeks!

Jesus: The end?

John
19 v 31-37

Today we're rejoining John's story of Jesus.

Jesus has died a tragic, lonely death.

But His story isn't over yet...

Could you tell the jury what happened on the night of the 16th?

I was walking by the bank, and I saw two men with masks...

A **witness** tells people what they saw, to convince them that something really happened. John witnessed Jesus' death.

Read John 19 v 35
Why has John told us what he saw?

So that _____

_____ (v35)

So what does John want us to believe? **Read verses 31-37**

John wants us to believe that Jesus really is the Son of God

He mentions two Old Testament prophecies about the Son of God, made hundreds of years before Jesus was around. They both happened to Jesus and prove He is the Son of God.

Draw lines to link up the Old Testament verses with what they say and with the verses where John mentions them.

Psalm 34 v 20	Zechariah 12 v 10
They'll look at the one who they pierced	None of his bones will be broken
John 19 v 36	John 19 v 37

John wants us to believe that Jesus really died

If Jesus didn't die, He couldn't have risen back to life and His whole message would have been a lie. *But find two pieces of **evidence** in verses 33-34...*

1. The cruel, leg-breaking soldiers made absolutely certain that Jesus was dead.

2. _____ and _____ came out of Jesus' side. That could only happen if Jesus were dead.

Think & pray!

So now you've read the evidence, do you really believe it all? Talk to God about your answer.

Tomb with a view

John
19 v 38-42

Not everyone wanted Jesus to die. Some people cared for him deeply.

*Use the **backwards** word pool to fill in the spaces throughout today's Discover page.*

rewollof   terces

ydob   nenil   hsiweJ

bmot   sumedociN   suseJ

hpesoJ   dellik   etaliP

aehtamirA   secips

Read John 19 v 38

J_____ from
A_____ was a
s_____ follower of
Jesus. He asked P_____
for Jesus' b_____.

Read verse 39

Joseph was helped by
N_____. This
man had once secretly
visited J_____ late at
night (see John 3 v 1-21). He
was a J_____ leader.
And it looks as if he had
become a f_____
of Jesus!

Read verses 40-42

The men put s_____ on
Jesus' body, and wrapped
it in l_____. They
put Jesus' body in a new
t_____, near where He
was k_____.

Think!

Not many people could have done that for Jesus. Write down things that only YOU can do for Jesus (e.g. telling a specific friend about Jesus).

_____

_____

_____

_____

Pray!

Read through the things you've written down. Ask God to give you the courage to do those things for Him.

WEIRD WORDS

Arimathea
A village 20 miles from Jerusalem

Pilate
The local governor (see Day 24)

Disciple
Follower

Myrrh/Aloes
Spices put on Jesus' body to stop it going nasty

Linen
Cloth

Tomb raiders

John 20 v 1-9

Jesus has died on the cross and been buried.

Surely that's the end of the story!

No way!

Fill in the gaps, using the word blocks, to complete an important verse from Matthew.

raised	third day	killed

suffer	disciples

Jesus began to explain to His _____ that he must go to Jerusalem and _____ many things at the hands of the elders, chief priests and teachers of the law, and that He must be _____ and on the _____ be _____ to life.
(Matthew 16 v 21)

Keep this verse in mind as you...
Read John 20 v 1-9

Mary assumed that grave robbers had swiped Jesus' body from the tomb. And Peter and John ("the one Jesus loved") were not expecting Jesus to be alive again!

But Jesus (and Old Testament Scriptures) had said this was going to happen! So why didn't they believe it?

Read verse 9 again
They hadn't fully understood what they'd read in God's Word.

Think!
Is the Bible sometimes like that to you? Maybe you've read or heard about Jesus loads of times. But do you really understand it?

Read verse 8 again

> **John s_____ and b_____**

John believed that Jesus' body had gone but didn't yet understand that Jesus had been raised back to life!

Think & pray!
Has it all become clear for you? Do you believe that Jesus died, and was raised back to life? If not, PRAY for God to help you to understand what Jesus has done for you.

Angel delight

**John
20 v 10-18**

*Mary Magdalene,
Peter and John
have discovered
that Jesus' body is
no longer in the
tomb.*

*And things are
about to get
even weirder for
Mary...*

WEIRD WORDS

Aramaic/Hebrew
Languages spoken by
Jewish people

Read John 20 v 10-13

1. Mary was crying because...

a) she had a headache ☐

b) Peter and John had
left her alone ☐

c) Jesus' body had gone ☐

Think!

What does this tell us about Mary's
love for Jesus? Do you love Jesus as
she did?

Read verses 14-15

2. Mary bumped into...

a) the gardener ☐

b) Jesus ☐

c) Peter and John ☐

Wow!

Mary wanted to find Jesus' body.
But she found far more than she'd
expected.

People who seek Jesus will never be
disappointed. And they'll get much
more than they hoped for.

Read verses 16-17

**3. Why didn't Jesus let Mary
cling to him?**

a) She hadn't believed him ☐

b) He didn't love her ☐

c) He was going to heaven ☐

Jesus was going back to be with His
Father in heaven, and He wanted
His disciples to know this.

Read verse 18

4. What did Mary do?

a) Went home for lunch ☐

b) Told the others about Jesus ☐

c) Kept her mouth shut ☐

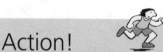

Action!

Jesus is alive! Don't you want to
tell your friends the great news?

Check your answers below. How
many mistakes did you make?

But a far more serious mistake is not
believing in the risen Jesus Christ.

Got that? Good.

Answers: 1-C 2-B 3-C 4-B
Mistakes: 0 = You're wise!
1 = You're wobbly!
2 = You're wubbish!

Free peace, sweet!

**John
20 v 19-23**

Jesus was cruelly killed on the cross.

But God amazingly raised Him back to life!

Which of these was a common greeting in New Testament times?

- **Nice to meet you**
- **Guten Morgen mein Freund**
- **Peace be with you!**
- **Wassup!**

Read today's Bible bit to find out...

Read John 20 v 19-21

Jesus was calmly greeting His friends who thought He was dead!

But Jesus really can bring us PEACE...
- **peace with God**
- **forgiveness for our sins**
- **rescue from punishment for our sin**

*But **how** can Jesus bring us peace? Fill in the vowels (aeiou) to complete Colossians 1 v 20.*

M__k__ng p__ __c__
thr__ __gh H__s bl__ __d
sh__d __n th__ cr__ss

By dying on the cross, and being raised back to life, Jesus has made it possible to be forgiven. To be at peace with God. We just have to trust in what He's done for us.

Those of us who've been forgiven by Jesus have a job to do...

Read verses 21-23

Wow!

That doesn't mean Christians have the power to forgive sins! It means they should be telling people what Jesus has done for them, by dying and coming back to life. Whether or not God forgives them depends on whether they accept Jesus.

And Jesus has given Christians His **Holy Spirit** to help them spread the great news! (v22)

Action!

1. If you're a Christian, who will you tell about Jesus?

_____

_____

Ask God to help you do it!

2. If you're not sure if you're a Christian, you might want to read the free e-booklet *What's it all about?* If so, email discover@thegoodbook.co.uk.

Believe it or not

John
20 v 24-31

Jesus has been raised back to life!

He has appeared to Mary and to His disciples.

But one disciple hasn't seen Jesus yet...

A Letters

B Letters

WEIRD WORDS

Messiah
The King who would rescue God's people

Read John 20 v 24-29
... and fill in the missing words.

Thomas was one of the

_ _ _ _ _ _ **disciples (v24).**
   A   A

He wouldn't believe Jesus was alive again unless he saw the marks left by the

_ _ _ _ _ **in Jesus'**
  A   A

hands, and put his

_ _ _ _ _ _ **into the**
B   A

holes, and his hand into Jesus' _ _ _ _ **(v25).**
      B   A

But when Thomas saw Jesus, he believed and said "My

_ _ _ _ _ **and my God!" (v28).**
B

Jesus said that people who believed in Him without having seen Him were

_ _ _ _ _ _ _ **(v29).**
  A   B

*Write down all the **A** and **B** letters in the box on the left.*

Wow!

The disciples had spent three years with Jesus, yet didn't realise that He was God's Son. But suddenly, for Thomas, it all made sense. Jesus is alive! He's beaten death! He is the Son of God!

It's awesome when it suddenly all makes sense. When someone finally realises that Jesus is God's Son. That He died for them. And that they can have all their sins forgiven by Him.

Read verses 30-31

*So why did John write a whole book about Jesus? Rearrange all the **A** letters from earlier to find the first word. Then the **B** letters for the second word.*

• **So that we will**

_ _ _ _ _ _ _

that Jesus is God's Son

• **So that we can have**

everlasting _ _ _ _

Think!

John wrote this book so that we'll believe in Jesus and go to live with Him forever.
Do you? Will you?

Something fishy

**John
21 v 1-14**

*What would
be your perfect
breakfast?*

_____

_____

_____

_____

Maybe a super-healthy bowl of muesli, topped with strawberries and a glass of pineapple juice? Or perhaps a lovely fry-up: bacon, sausage, eggs, hash browns, mushrooms, the works?

Today we'll see the disciples tuck into an unusual fry-up on the beach. Mmmm... tasty.

Read John 21 v 1-3

After a whole night's fishing, how many fish had they caught?

That's a bit surprising. These guys were expert fishermen!

Read verses 4-8

They may have been good fishermen, but they couldn't do it on their own this time!

Fill in the missing letters to reveal something Jesus had said to His disciples earlier.

W__th__ __t m__
y__u c__n d__
n__th__ng
(John 15 v 5)

Action!

What are you good at?

_____

What do you do to serve God?

_____

_____

Do you ask the Lord to help you or do you try to do stuff by yourself? Why not try asking God to help you whenever you start something new?

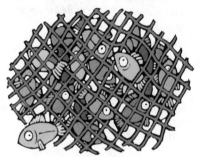

Now read verses 9-14

The disciples must have been so hungry after being out all night on the boat. Amazing! The Lord Jesus fried a breakfast for His disciples!

Pray!

Thank Jesus that He cares for His followers (Christians). He provides just what they need at the right time. It's dumb to try to do stuff without Him!

Question time

John
21 v 15-17

You've messed up this time.

You were only messing about, but you've managed to smash your mum's favourite ornament.

It doesn't look too good now with a huge crack in it!

You're sat at the dinner table and you know that she knows. You're trying to work out what that look means. *"Is she really angry? How bad is it? Have I been forgiven?"*

Do you know that feeling?

Peter must have been feeling a bit like that. This was the third time Peter had met Jesus since his dreadful denials. And Jesus hadn't mentioned it... yet.

Read John 21 v 15-17

How many times had Peter denied knowing Jesus?

How many times did Jesus ask Peter this question?

Now fill in the speech bubbles from verse 16.

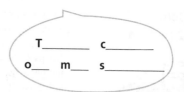

T_____ c_____
o___ m___ s_____

What's all this sheep feeding stuff?

Jesus gave Peter the special job of looking after His sheep. That means looking after Jesus' followers. Great!

Now put yourself in Peter's shoes. Jesus asks you: **"Do you love me?"** What's YOUR answer?

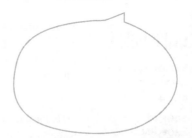

WEIRD WORDS

Simon Peter/ Peter/Simon
All the same person, who had pretended not to know Jesus (John 18 v 25-27)

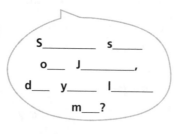

S_____ s_____
o___ J_____,
d___ y_____ I_____
m___?

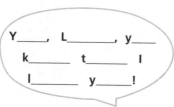

Y_____, L_____, y_____
k_____ t_____ I
I_____ y_____!

Pray!

If you love Jesus, and have had your wrongs forgiven by Him... He wants you to serve Him, as Peter did. Tell Jesus how much you love Him, and ask Him to help you serve Him with your life.

Follow the leader

John
21 v 18-25

Today is our last look at John's story of Jesus.

And Jesus has one final thing to say to Peter.

Today's answers can all be found in the wordsearch.

N	S	B	J	P	G	O	D	F
C	U	E	T	W	B	V	I	X
F	O	L	L	O	W	G	E	S
Y	L	I	F	E	B	E	C	T
H	E	E	H	P	E	T	E	R
E	A	V	S	U	S	E	J	E
S	D	E	G	L	O	R	Y	T
O	K	G	A	Z	L	D	R	C
N	D	L	Q	S	D	N	A	H

Read John 21 v 18-19

"When you are o_____,

you will s_____

out your h_____ and

someone else will dress you

and l_____ you where

you don't want to go".

Jesus said this to show

P_____ that he would

d_____ on a cross and

bring g_____ to God.

Then Jesus said

"F_____ me!"

Wow!

Following Jesus will lead to tough times: teasing, loneliness, bullying. In some countries, people are even killed for following Jesus.

Pray!

Pray for Christians in countries where they are given a really hard time. Places like Somalia, Iraq, North Korea and Nigeria.

Read verses 20-23

Jesus told Peter not to worry about John, but to concentrate on serving God.

Read verses 24-25

John couldn't possibly tell us all the amazing things Jesus did. It would take forever!

Remember why John wrote this book? (Clue: look at John 20 v 31)

So that you b_____

that J_____ is the

S_____ of G_____, and have

everlasting l_____.

We've reached the end of John's book. Do you believe that Jesus is God's Son, or do you need to do more thinking?

WEIRD WORDS

Glorify God
Bring honour to God

The believers
All the followers of Jesus

Testifies
Tells everyone

Testimony
Evidence

Romans: Only one way

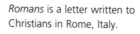

Romans
1 v 1-7

Romans is a letter written to Christians in Rome, Italy.

We're about to read an incredible book called Romans.

Prepare to be amazed...

Who wrote it?

Read Romans 1 v 1

P_____ did. He was a s_____ of J_____. He was an ap_____. **That means he was sent by God to tell people about Jesus.**

This is the same Paul that you can read about in the book of Acts. Paul wrote to these Christians because he couldn't visit them.

Read verse 5

God sent out people like Paul to tell everyone this good news about Jesus, so that they would trust Jesus and obey Him.

Who was the letter to?

Read verses 6-7

To people in Rome who followed J_____ Ch_____. Paul calls them holy people (your Bible might say "saints"). That means they are *set apart by God* to serve Him.

What is it about?

Read verses 2-4

The g_____ (v2). That's God's good news that Jesus can rescue us from our sinful ways. It's all about Jesus who is God's S_____ (v3). He became a hu_____n (v3) and had God's Sp_____ with Him (v4). He died on the cross and God raised Him back to life (v4).

Wow!

If you're a follower of Jesus, you're one of his holy people too! You are set apart by God to serve Him. This letter is for YOU too!

Pray!

Thank God that this good news is for you. Ask Him to help you understand what He wants to teach you in Romans.

Wish I was there

**Romans
1 v 8-13**

*Paul is writing
a letter to the
Christians in
Rome.*

*It's full of the
good news
about Jesus.*

*Hope to see you soon,
love Rach xxx*

Do you ever end emails or letters like that? *See you soon!*

Paul is so keen on visiting these Christians in Rome that it's one of the **first** things he says. Check out **verse 11**.

"I long to see you."

Paul didn't even know most of these people! Why was he so keen to meet them?

Read Romans 1 v 8-13

Complete the reasons by using the right letter blocks.

WEIRD WORDS

Faith
Their trust in God

Impart
Give, share

Mutually
Both

Harvest
People becoming
Christians

ports	**pray**	**aith**
	encour	**encou**
streng	**const**	

1. Paul had heard good re_____ about their f_____ (v8).

2. He'd been praying for them _____antly. He wanted to see how his _____ers were being answered (v9-10).

3. Paul had wanted to help and _____then them by _____aging them (v11-12).

4. He wanted to be _____raged by spending time with them (v12).

Think!

Do you meet up with other Christians regularly or do you avoid them?

Wow!

Meeting up with Christians your age can be encouraging (and fun). You can share your thoughts and experiences. You can pray for each other. And talking to older believers can be great too. You can learn from them.

Action!

Which Christians could you spend more time with?

_____

Will you pluck up the courage?

Ashamed of Jesus?

Romans
1 v 14-17

In his letter to the Christians in Rome, Paul starts to get personal...

He tells them 3 important things about himself.

To discover them, fill in the missing Es as you read the verses.

Read Romans 1 v 14

1. I am a debtor to both Gr__ __ks and non-Gr__ __ks

That means that Paul wants to tell the gospel to everyone. It doesn't matter whether they speak Greek or not. It doesn't matter if they are intelligent or not so clever. **Everyone** needs to hear about Jesus!

Wow!

God sent His Son Jesus to die in our place so that our wrongs can be forgiven. We know this, so we should tell other people about it too. We owe it to God. And we owe it to people who don't know Jesus.

Read verse 15

2. I am so __ag__r to pr__ach the gosp__l to you

Are you desperate to tell your friends that Jesus died for them? Do you want them to believe in Jesus? To be saved by Him and live for Him?

Read verses 16-17

3. I am not asham__d of the gosp__l

Why wasn't Paul ashamed?

The gosp__l is the pow__r of God to save __v__ryon__ who b__li__v__s

This great news about Jesus can save people from their sinful ways if they believe in Him! Why be embarrassed about **that**?!

Think!

Are you embarrassed to tell your friends or family the good news about Jesus? Who should you tell about Jesus?

_____

_____

Pray!

Ask God to help you be ready and willing to talk to your friends about Jesus and what you've learned in the Bible. Now go and do it!

For a free e-booklet called *How Do I Show I'm A Christian?*, email discover@thegoodbook.co.uk or check out www.thegoodbook.co.uk/contact-us to find our UK mailing address.

No excuses!

**Romans
1 v 18-27**

Read Romans 1 v 18-20

God is angry with people who disobey Him. But is it fair that God is angry with people who haven't been told about Him? *Complete the answer from v20.*

EVERYONE...

- can see God's cr__ __ti__n.
  We can all see the amazing world God has made.
- knows deep down that only G__d has the p__w__r to create life.
- is without any exc__s__ for disobeying God.

Read verses 21-23

That's why God has every right to be angry with people who disobey Him and put other things ahead of Him. God shows His anger by letting people do all the bad things they want to.

That doesn't sound too bad, does it? But they have to suffer the results of their sin too.

*Draw arrows from each of the **sins** to the **results** of that sin. Draw as many as you like.*

greed	violence
hatred	hurt
lying	stealing
cheating	fear
violence	emptiness

Paul uses an example to show us why God is angry when people reject Him. Because sin messes up the world.

Read verses 24-27

Because people rebelled against God, husbands and wives are tempted to do wrong. So God's punishment was to let them follow their twisted desire for sin — all kinds of wrong sexual relationships, including homosexuality. So they must suffer the results of their sins: marriage break-ups, misery, sexually transmitted infections.

Many awful things like this are the result of people rejecting God and choosing not to live His way.

Pray!

Say sorry to God for specific times you've let Him down. Ask Him to help you obey Him more and more.

Any questions on this tricky subject? Email us: discover@thegoodbook.co.uk

Rotten list

**Romans
1 v 28-32**

*Paul is still
telling us how
angry God is
with people
who refuse to
live for Him.*

Read Romans 1 v 28

We all have the fantastic chance
to **know God**. To have a personal
relationship with Him! Sadly, many
people turn their backs on God and
refuse to know Him.

*Write a **Rotten List** of the wrong
things people do because they have
rejected God.*

Now read verses 29-31

*Tick the things on your list that Paul
mentions. Add any that you missed.
(Use a dictionary if you need to!)*

We can feel really bad when we
do any of these things. But not
everyone feels bad about it.

Read verse 32

No one has an excuse. Everyone
knows what's right and wrong. We
know that God punishes people
who reject Him. Yet many people
are **happy** to do wrong and even
encourage sinning!

Wow!

Don't get too down! This letter to
the Romans wasn't written just to
show how rotten we are. It was
written to tell us that even the worst
of us can be forgiven by God!

WEIRD WORDS

Retain
Keep

Depraved
Sinful

Strife
Fighting

Malice
Wanting to harm
someone

Slanderers
They lie about other
people

Insolent
Disrespectful

Fidelity
Faithfulness

Righteous decree
Perfect law

Rotten List

Prayer action!

Think of friends and family who
refuse to know God. Write all
their names on a piece of paper.
Every day, will you ask God to
save them from their wrong
ways?

Judge dread

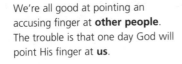

**Romans
2 v 1-10**

Josh is such a liar! He's always making stuff up.

We're all good at pointing an accusing finger at **other people**. The trouble is that one day God will point His finger at **us**.

Read Romans 2 v 1-3

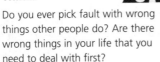

Think!
Do you ever pick fault with wrong things other people do? Are there wrong things in your life that you need to deal with first?

Read verses 4-6
Paul is talking to Jewish people who often thought they were better than the Gentiles (non-Jews). Yet they didn't try to get rid of the sin in their lives. They thought God was soft and wouldn't punish them (v4).

But God gives us **all** the chance to stop sinning and to live for Him (v4). Those who don't will one day be judged and punished for disobeying God (v5-6).

Read verses 8-9
What are the results of doing wrong? Unjumble to find out.

w_____
t h r a w

t_____
b l o u t e r

a_____
g r e a n

p_____
n a p i

What about people who obey God, turn to Jesus and have their wrongs forgiven?

Read verses 7 & 10

g_____
l y r o g

h_____
r u n h o o

p_____
e c a p e

e_____ l____
r e n t a l e   f i l e

Wow!

God is not ignoring us. He knows everything we do, think and say. One day, He will punish everyone who disobeys Him. But those who have had their wrongs forgiven by Jesus will have glory, honour and peace for eternity!

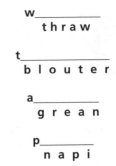

WEIRD WORDS

Condemning
Showing yourself to be guilty

Contempt
Lack of respect

Repentance
Turning away from sin

Forbearance
Tolerance

Stubbornness
Refusing to change

Wrath
Anger

Immortality
Living forever

No favourites

**Romans
2 v 11-16**

*Who are your
favourite people?*

_____

_____

_____

_____

Does God have favourites? Who will God look most favourably on at the day of His judgment?

> **Jews**
> who had the great privilege of being taught God's laws?

or

> **Gentiles**
> who'd had no teaching about God's truth?

Is God more likely to forgive...

> **Me and you**
> who have read or heard at least some of the Bible and know a bit about Jesus?

or

> **Other people**
> who know nothing about Jesus or what the Bible says?

Read the answer in...

Romans 2 v 11

There's no excuse for anyone, because we all know that we've done wrong...

Read verses 12-13

We are a lot like these Jewish people, because we also have God's law written in the Bible.

It tells us what's right and wrong. So we have **no excuse** for doing wrong.

People with no Bible are like the Gentiles. But God's law is written on their hearts (v15).

Their conscience tells them what's right and wrong. They too have no excuse.

Now it should be easier to understand today's Romans bit.

Read verses 12-16 carefully

Wow!

We have all done wrong, and we'll all be judged for what we've done. The only way to avoid God's punishment is to trust Jesus and what He's done to save us.

WEIRD WORDS

Perish
Die

Righteous
Right with God

Bearing witness
Giving evidence

Inside out?

**Romans
2 v 17-29**

Many Jewish leaders were hypocrites. They bragged about being close to God and knowing His will (what He wanted). But they didn't actually **live God's way**. Paul told them to practice what they preached!

Read Romans 2 v 17-22

Think!

Are you ever like those guys? Proud of what you know from the Bible? Critical when someone else does wrong? Not always great at actually doing what God's Word says?

Read verses 23-24

How can we claim to be Christians if we don't live God's way? When people notice what hypocrites we are, it makes God look bad too!

Read verses 28-29

Paul said there were two kinds of Jew. Two different ways of living.

God's people are those who really **love and follow** Him. Like the inward Jew. But to do that we need our hearts changed by God (v29).

Read verses 25-27

Circumcision was the sign of being a Jew, one of God's people. But what good was it if a circumcised Jew didn't live for God?

Paul said that Gentiles (non-Jews) could be God's people even though they hadn't been circumcised.

You're not one of God's people just because you go to church or have a Christian family. God's not interested in what we're like on the outside. What counts is this: **Has your heart been changed?**

Outward Jews
- Have been **circumcised**
- **Know** God's law
- **Think** they please God

Inward Jews
- **Heart** changed by God
- **Obey** God's law
- **Really** please God

Action!

How can you practice what you preach this week?
(eg: obeying your parents)

_____

_____

_____

Ask God to help you!

What's the point???

**Romans
3 v 1-4**

I've got the worst of both worlds! Having a Christian family doesn't make me a Christian, so that's no help. But I can't enjoy life like everyone else, because I feel bad when I do wrong stuff!

So far, Paul's told us that God is angry with our sin and will punish us for it.

We have no excuses for disobeying God.

Even God's special people (Jews) had to trust in Jesus to be forgiven. Just being a Jew or going to church wasn't enough.

Some of the Jews in Paul's time were having similar thoughts. They had God's law and they had been circumcised. But now Paul was saying that those things didn't make you right with God.

So what was the point of being a Jew? It seemed to be no advantage at all. But Paul knew better.

Read Romans 3 v 1-2

There were many advantages in being a Jew. And there are many advantages in having a Christian family. *Add some to the list...*

1. They steer you away from bad influences

2. They pray for you

3.

4.

5.

We're so privileged because we have been taught so much about God too (v2). We understand that Jesus died to take the punishment for our wrongs.

Pray!

Thank God that you learn loads from His Word, the Bible.

Maybe you're thinking...

Most people don't believe in God. Surely they can't all be wrong!

Paul had an answer for arguments like that.

Read verses 3-4

Even if everyone refused to believe, they would all be...

RIGHT/WRONG _____

And God would be...

RIGHT/WRONG _____

WEIRD WORDS

Nullify
Cancel out

Faithfulness
Keeping promises

Prevail
Succeed

Wow!

Paul was saying that we all fail to obey God. But that doesn't mean God won't keep His fantastic promises to us.
Read some of them...
Psalm 111 v 4-9
John 3 v 16
Acts 2 v 38-39

Twisting the truth

**Romans
3 v 5-8**

Which of these shows up more clearly?

GOD IS GOOD

or

GOD IS GOOD

The black background shows up **GOD IS GOOD** better. Now imagine that **sin** is a bit like the black background. Our sin makes God's goodness stand out much brighter than if we were perfect like Him.

That's true, but Paul knows that some people jump to the wrong conclusion. They hate his teaching about God punishing sin. And they want to find an excuse for their sin.

Follow the argument Paul has with such people. *Read the verses when they're mentioned.*

Read Romans 3 v 5

If our sin shows up God's goodness, then we're doing Him a favour by sinning! So how can God be fair to punish us for our sin?

Read verse 6

That's an awful thing to suggest. Sin is **disobeying God**, so God will **punish** people who sin.

Read verses 7-8

But God's truth looks much brighter compared to my sin. So God can't punish me for sinning. Let's sin more, so that God's goodness looks even better!

End of verse 8

People who say such evil, twisted things will receive the **punishment** they deserve.

We shouldn't make excuses for the wrong stuff we do. It's **always** wrong to disobey God. He will punish everyone who sins, unless they have been **forgiven by Jesus**.

Pray!

Is there anything you need to say sorry to God for?

WEIRD WORDS

Unrighteousness
Sin, disobedience to God

Righteousness
Living God's way

Unjust
Unfair

Wrath
God's anger and punishment

Falsehood
Lies

Enhances
Makes it seem even better

Slanderously
People told lies about them

Condemnation
Punishment for sinning against God

No one's perfect

Romans
3 v 9-20

Imagine being all alone on a desert island.

No one to tempt you to sin. No one to annoy you either!

WEIRD WORDS

Open graves
Unclean and impure, like open graves

Deceit
Lying, deceiving

Accountable
Responsible and deserving to be punished for any sin

Works of the law
Keeping God's law

Conscious
Aware

Do you think you'd be perfect and godly on your own?

YES/NO _____

Paul tells us that **none** of us is perfect. We all naturally do wrong. Only God can change us so that we're more like Him.

Read Romans 3 v 9-20

*Put these phrases into the right boxes to show **what we're all like** and **what none of us is like**. Use the verses to help you.*

worthless (v12)

righteous (right with God) (v10)

seeks God (v11)

lies with their tongues (v13)

full of cursing (v14)

understands God (v11)

bitter (v14)

violent (v15)

does good (v12)

peaceful (v17)

fears God (v18)

miserable (v16)

What everyone is naturally like
1.
2.
3.
4.
5.
6.

That includes us. But we don't have to stay sinful. Tomorrow, Paul will show us how we can be rescued!

What no one is naturally like
1.
2.
3.
4.
5.
6.

Nobody is naturally like this. But GOD can change us to become like that and live for Him. Have you had your life changed by God?

Pray!

We can't live perfect lives. We stuff things up. But thank God that He has given us another way to please Him. We'll read about it tomorrow.

God's great gift

**Romans
3 v 21-26**

*Paul has just
told us that
EVERYONE is
sinful and will
be punished by
God.*

*But Paul has
some great
news...*

Imagine this. Your dad says he'll buy you a iPhone... but only if you get rid of **every** weed in your massive garden. You start straight away, but soon realise it's an **IMPOSSIBLE** task. As soon as you've killed half of the weeds, more have sprung up in their place.

But there's **GREAT NEWS**. Your dad says he'll do the job for you, totally free, without you having to lift a finger. And you can still have the iPhone!

That's a tiny bit like what God has done for us. We try to earn our way to eternal life by living good lives. We want to obey God, but we find it **IMPOSSIBLE** to get rid of all our sin.

But there's **GREAT NEWS!** God has offered to forgive all our sin. For free. And we don't have to do anything. God sent His Son Jesus to rescue us!

Read Romans 3 v 21-26

It's hard stuff to understand. So let's look at it more closely.

Read verse 22

We can have all our sins forgiven by Jesus. We just have to rely on His death in our place and trust Him to forgive us.

Read verse 24

We can be **justified**. That means we're declared **not guilty** by God because our sins have been forgiven.

It's a **free** gift, even though we deserve to be punished in hell. This is God's **grace**.

We can be forgiven because of the **redemption that came from Jesus.** That means Jesus paid the price for our sins. He took the punishment we deserve. He died on the cross in our place! Wow!

WEIRD WORDS

Righteousness
Being right with God, forgiven

Law and the Prophets testify
Means, "the Old Testament says..."

Sacrifice of atonement
Jesus died on the cross to take our punishment

Pray!

Jesus is the one we need. There is no catch. He has made forgiveness totally free. Is there anything you want to say to Him?

Faith the facts

Romans

3 v 27-31

Paul has told us that everyone has sinned and deserves to be punished by God.

But God sent His Son Jesus, who took the punishment in our place.

If we trust Him to, He will forgive our sins!

WEIRD WORDS

Excluded
Not included

Works of the law
Keeping the law

Nullify
Cancel

Uphold it
Keep it

How can God forgive useless sinners like us?! Is it because of anything **we** do to please God?

YES/NO _____

No, we can't live perfect lives that please God. Paul tells us we are acceptable to God because of... (the answer appears five times in verses 27-31)

F __ __ __ __

That means relying on Jesus for forgiveness

Now Paul answers three questions about being forgiven by Jesus. *Read the verses and fill in the missing words.*

Read Romans 3 v 27-28

> **Can we bo_____ about having our sins forgiven?**

> No! We can't b_____t about that, because we haven't done anything. J_____ did it all by dying on the cross to take the punishment we deserve. We just have to trust in His forgiveness.

Read verses 29-30

> **Is God's great news just for J_____ or is it for G_____ too?**

> God offers forgiveness to everyone. There is only one G_____. So there is only one way to be saved from our sins: faith in Jesus. That is true for EVERYONE!

Read verse 31

> **Do we get rid of the l_____ by this faith?**

Or in other words...

> **Can we trust in Jesus but carry on living our own way?**

> No chance! We've been forgiven by God, so we should try to live His way, obeying Him. Not live for ourselves, but for God.

Pray!

Ask God to help you...
a) not boast about being a Christian
b) tell others about Jesus
c) live your life for God

Abraham link on

Romans
4 v 1-8

Paul has told us that nothing we do can put us right with God.

Only JESUS can forgive our sins.

Need convincing? Well, Paul's determined to make us understand! *Use the backwards word pool to complete the explanations.*

> develieb   segaw
> tfig   denrae   tnuoc
> desselB   nevigrof   snis
> maharbA   skrow   tsaob
> erutpircS   divaD   htiaf
> tsurt   dekciw

Read Romans 4 v 1-3

Many people think that if they live good enough lives, they will go to be with God in heaven. But we're all sinful — we **can't** be good enough for God. Even Abraham didn't live a good enough life!

A_____ was not justified by w_____ (v2). He had nothing to b_____ about (v2). The S_____ says that Abraham b_____ God (v3), and that's why God accepted him. It wasn't down to Abraham's good deeds, but because he *believed* God and trusted Him.

Read verses 4-5

When you work, your w_____ are not given to you as a g_____. You have e_____ them (v4). But we can't earn forgiveness and being put right with God. Amazingly, God justifies (forgives) w_____ people who t_____ God (v5). They're put right with God because of their f_____ in Him (v5). It's all down to God, not us!

Read verses 6-8

King D_____ (v6) said the same thing in Psalm 32. He said "Blessed are they whose s_____ are f_____ (v7)." "B_____ is the one whose sin God won't c_____ against them (v8)."

Pray!

If you mean it, admit to God that you're not good enough to be with Him. Now thank God that if you trust in Jesus, your sins are forgiven! God won't count them against you!

Showing promise

**Romans
4 v 9-17**

*Paul is still
telling us about
Abraham...*

Some people thought...

> **Abraham was right
> with God (justified)
> because he was
> circumcised.**

What does Paul say?

Read Romans 4 v 9-12

> **Rubbish! Abraham
> was circumcised as a SIGN
> that he was right with
> God. It was to show that
> he BELONGED to God.
> Circumcision doesn't put
> things right with God.**

God made some great promises
to Abraham. Find some of them in
Genesis 12 v 1-3. Jot them down.

God's promises

Now read Romans 4 v 13-15
Abraham didn't receive these
promises because he obeyed God's
law. It was because of his faith
in God. It was a gift from God.
Abraham didn't earn it.

Read verses 16-17

Wow!
God's promise to Abraham is for
ALL BELIEVERS!

He promised that Abraham would
be the father of many nations. That
promise means that ANYONE can be
part of God's people, not just the
Israelites.

We don't deserve to be God's
people — it's an undeserved gift
(grace)!

Pray!

Thank God that we don't have
to earn His love and forgiveness.
Thank Him that it's an undeserved
gift to anyone who accepts it.
Pray for people you know who
haven't yet accepted God's gift.

Believe it or not?

Romans 4 v 18-25

"We'll win this match!" your coach promises.

But you're losing 3-0, half your team is injured and the other side are HUGE!

Do you believe the promise?

YES/NO _____

WEIRD WORDS

Justification
To put us right with God. Jesus made it possible for our sins to be forgiven!

Abraham had an even harder promise to believe. Find God's unbelievable promise to Abraham in **Romans 4 v 17**.

> I have made you a
> f_____ of many
> n_____

But it didn't seem very likely...
Read Romans 4 v 18-21

The facts (v19)

1. Abraham's b_____ was as good as d_____
2. He was about _____ years old
3. His wife S_____ was unable to have children

How could they have children?! How could Abraham have a huge family? But nothing is impossible for God!

Abraham's great faith

• Against all hope, Abraham b_____ (v18)
• He was strengthened in his f_____ and gave glory to G____ (v20)
• He believed God would keep His p_____ (v21)

Abraham trusted God to keep His promise and He did! That's great news for us too...

Read verses 22-25

God's promise to us

• God sent J_____ to rescue us
• He was handed over to d_____ for our s_____ (v25)
• God r_____ Jesus back to l_____ (v25)
• God promises that everyone who believes that Jesus died in their place can have their sins forgiven!

Think!

Do you believe God's promise? Have you done anything about it? For the free e-booklet about Jesus called *What's it all about?* email discover@thegoodbook.co.uk or check out www.thegoodbook.co.uk/contact-us to find our UK mailing address.

Numbers: Count on God

Numbers
20 v 1-13

Today we're turning to the book of **Numbers** to join Moses and the Israelites in the desert.

The story so far...

• God rescued Moses and the Israelites from slavery in Egypt

• He was guiding them to a new place to live — Canaan

• But the people kept disobeying God and turning away from Him

• So God punished them by making them wander round the desert for 40 years

Read Numbers 20 v 1-5

Cross out the Bs, Cs and Ds to show what the people did wrong.

CBQUDDARCDREBCLLDCB
INDGWCITBBHMCDOSBES

_ _ _ _ _ _ _ _ _ _ _

_ _ _ _   _ _ _ _ _

WEIRD WORDS

Israelites
The nation God chose to be His special people

Miriam
Moses' sister

Livestock
Animals

Pomegranates
Fruit with loads of seeds

Assembly
Everyone

Tent of Meeting
Tent where God was present

Glory of the Lord
What God is like

Staff
Special stick

Holy
Perfect, pure

The people were moaning at Moses and God because they were thirsty. They didn't trust God to help them.

Read verses 6-13

God gave the grumbling Israelites the water they wanted. But what did Moses do wrong?

For 39 years Moses had...
put up with the people's grumbling and disobedience

Now he... (pick one)
a) refused to help them
b) was still very patient
c) lost his temper

For 39 years Moses had...
trusted God completely

Now he... (pick two)
a) hit the rock instead of speaking
b) willingly obeyed God
c) didn't fully trust God

Moses and Aaron disobeyed God's orders and dishonoured Him, so God punished them (v12). Like the rest of their generation, they would not get to live in the promised land of Canaan.

Pray!

Say sorry to God for specific times you've not trusted Him. Ask God to help you to trust Him and obey Him.

Family war tunes

**Numbers
20 v 14-21**

*The Lord is
leading His
people (the
Israelites) to
the land He has
promised them
— Canaan.*

Take a look at the map.

The arrow shows the route they
wanted to take.

**If they went that way, they
would have to pass through
the unfriendly country of**

— — — —

What would you do?

Attack Edom ☐

Ask politely if you
could pass through ☐

Find another route ☐

Read Numbers 20 v 14-21

… to see what the Israelites decided
to do.

Israel claimed to be Edom's

b _ _ _ _ _ _ (v14).

To work out what they meant,
check out **Genesis 25 v 24-26.**

**Jacob and Esau were
brothers**

**Jacob's descendants
became Israel**

**Esau's descendants
became Edom**

**So Israel and Edom
were like brothers**

But the Edomites wouldn't let the
Israelites cross their land.

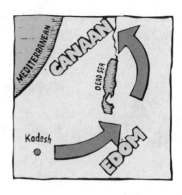

Kadesh

What would you do?

Attack Edom ☐

Ask politely if you
could pass through ☐

Find another route ☐

In the same way, people will get
in the way of Christians when they
try to follow Jesus. Sometimes the
opposition comes from people
we don't expect — even our own
families!

The Israelites wisely took the
decision to avoid a fight and took
the long route around Edom.

Action!

When you get opposition for
being a Christian, don't go
crazy. Ask God to help you
remain calm and do things His
way. Even if it means taking a
more difficult route.

Family gathering

**Numbers
20 v 22-29**

*Both Moses and
Aaron disobeyed
God, by not
following His
commands.*

*That's really
serious.*

*Now Aaron will
be punished...*

Read Numbers 20 v 22-29

*How do you think Aaron felt (v24)?
Circle your answers.*

disappointed

happy

frightened

upset

confused

relieved

angry

not bothered

Aaron must have been so
disappointed. But even though God
was punishing him, there was still
some hope for him...

Look at verse 26 again

Gathered to his people

That means Aaron would die, but he
would go to live with God for ever.
And so will everyone who trusts in
God to rescue them from their sins.

Imagine if your dad was also your
teacher at school. When you did
something wrong, it would be him
who had to punish you.

But when you go home, he's **still
your dad**. The two of you are still
in the same family and you can still
enjoy each other's company.

Wow!

When Christians do wrong, they
upset God. And they should say
sorry to Him.

But it doesn't change the fact that
He loves them and will be with them
for ever!

WEIRD WORDS

Edom
Country that
wouldn't let the
Israelites pass
through

Garments
Clothes

Mourned
Were very upset

Aaron will be with God for ever.
Even though God had to punish
Aaron, it didn't mean the end of
their relationship.

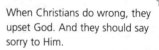

Pray!

Read **Romans 8 v 38-39**. How
amazing is that?! Thank God for
this fantastic truth about His love
for us.

Snakes alive!

**Numbers
21 v 1-9**

The Israelites keep turning against God, even though He's done so many amazing things for them.

Surely by now they've learned the lesson to trust God and obey Him...

WEIRD WORDS

Canaanite
From the land of Canaan

The Negev
The Negev desert

Vow
Promise

Hormah
The name means destruction

Read Numbers 21 v 1-3

The Israelites came up against the king of Arad's army. This time the people trusted God to give them victory. And He did!

But it wasn't long before the Israelites were back to their sinful, complaining ways...

Read verses 4-7

God rightly punished the people for turning against Him. Use the word pool to fill in the blanks.

> death   whole
> poisoned
> nothing   rid

The snakes had _____ the people. There was no way of getting _____ of the poison because it affected the _____ of their bodies. There was _____ they could do; poison meant certain _____.

Only God could cure them.

Read verses 8-9

… to see His cure.

The people turned towards the snake to be healed.

*Jesus saves us from our **sin** in a similar way. Use the word pool words again here...*

Sin has _____ each of us. It's impossible to get _____ of it because it has affected the _____ of our lives. There is _____ we can do; sin means certain _____.

Only Jesus can save us.

Read John 3 v 14-16.

We have to turn to Jesus to be saved from our sin.

Think & pray!

Have you turned to Jesus yet? Have you asked Him to forgive you and trusted Him to do it? Talk to God about it now.

For free info about becoming a Christian, email discover@thegoodbook.co.uk or check out www.thegoodbook.co.uk/contact-us to find our UK mailing address.

Giving thanks

Numbers
21 v 10-20

Moses and the Israelites are heading for the promised land — Canaan.

And they're getting closer...

Read Numbers 21 v 10-15

In the wordsearch, find eight of the places on their travels. The map will help you.

A	S	N	S	O	H	Z	T	V
R	Z	L	Z	K	C	E	D	R
I	Y	E	A	B	A	R	I	M
S	L	U	H	G	Y	E	N	A
U	Q	K	A	B	F	D	J	F
P	G	O	B	O	T	H	U	M
H	P	D	T	Y	Z	I	C	O
A	R	N	O	N	E	O	X	A
H	O	X	B	E	H	V	A	B

The Israelites were finally rushing towards the land God had promised them. And God was looking after them...

Read verse 16

God gave them w_____

No big deal, right? Well look back at **Numbers 20 v 5 and 21 v 5**. Then fill in what the people were whining about.

> **There is no w_____!**

Despite their complaining, God looked after His people and kept them alive. And this time, the Israelites reacted in the right way.

WEIRD WORDS

Moab
This country was an enemy of the Israelites

Ravines
Narrow valleys

Nobles
Rich and important people

Sceptres/staffs
Poles/sticks that important and powerful people carried

Read Numbers 21 v 17-20
They praised God for what He had done for them.

Think!
Scribble down some of the things God has done for you.

_____

_____

_____

_____

_____

_____

_____

Pray!

Spend time praising God and thanking Him for those things. God is great!

Fighting talk

**Numbers
21 v 21-35**

*The Israelites
are well on their
way to Canaan,
the land God
promised them.*

*But not
everyone wants
them to get
there...*

Read Numbers 21 v 21-22
The Israelites wanted to pass
peacefully through this country.
*Underline the things they promised
to do.*

Stay on the king's highway

Pollute all the water

Set fire to the fields

Not go into any vineyards

Not steal any water

Play hockey in vineyards

But the Amorites wouldn't make
things easy for the Israelites.

Read verse 23
*Would King Sihon let Israel pass
through his land?*

YES/ NO _____

**Now read verses 24-31 to see
what happened.**
King Sihon wanted to destroy the
Israelites but God's people defeated
King Sihon's army. And that wasn't
the end of the fighting.

Read verses 32-35
*Who made sure the Israelites won
all their battles?*

The L_____ (v34)

Wow!
God was looking after His people. If
you are a Christian, then you're one
of God's people. He's looking after
you too!

Pray!

Thank God that He looks after
His people. Ask Him to give
you the courage to live for Him,
even if people try to get in your
way, making things hard for you
because you're a Christian.

Balak, Balaam, Blessing

**Numbers
22 v 1-12**

King Balak

Now the action switches to the country of Moab, one of Israel's enemies.

Read Numbers 22 v 1-6

Who's who?

Is_____s (v1)
God's people, on their way to Canaan. God is giving them victory over every enemy they face.

M_____s (v4)
People from the country of Moab. Enemies of God and the Israelites.

B_____ (v4)
Evil king of Moab. He is scared that the Israelites will defeat his army.

B_____ (v5)
A diviner. That's someone who tries to predict the future. Balaam is not on God's side (yet).

King Balak knew that his army stood no chance against Israel. So he asked Balaam to put a curse on the Israelites.

Look back at Genesis 12 v 1-3

God promised Abram three great things:

1. Abram's descendants would become a **GREAT NATION** (the Israelites).

2. They would have a great **LAND** to live in (Canaan).

3. They would be **BLESSED** by God and all nations would be blessed through them.

Let's see if God kept His promises...

1. Numbers 22 v 5 shows that God's people had become a **GREAT NATION**.

2. They were on their way to Canaan, the **PROMISED LAND**.

3. God gave them great **BLESSINGS**. And one day, Jesus would be a descendant of Abram. He would make it possible for people of all nations to be with God!

The Israelites really were blessed!

Pray!

Thank God that He is so good to His people. And that His blessing can't be taken away from us by anyone.

WEIRD WORDS

The Jordan
A huge, impressive river

Jericho
Important city

Horde
Huge number of people

Fee for divination
What Balaam was paid for the evil magic they wanted him to use

Read verses 7-12

Balaam didn't serve God. Yet God was going to use him to help the Israelites. Balaam couldn't curse God's people because they were **blessed** (v12). That means God had promised really good things to His people.

Verses 13-20 show us that so far, Balaam is doing exactly what God tells him to. Or is he? Find out tomorrow...

What a donkey!

**Numbers
22 v 21-41**

Balaam

Balak the king
of Moab is
worried that the
Israelites will
defeat his army.

So he's asked
Balaam to put
a curse on the
Israelites.

Balaam is on his way to meet King
Balak. He seems to be following
God's orders, but God knows that
Balaam is only serving himself.
Balaam needs a reminder of who's
in charge...

Read Numbers 22 v 21-27

Balaam is the real donkey! He can't
see what God is doing. He is blind
to spiritual things — things to do
with God.

Pray!

Write down the names of people
you know who seem to be blind to
spiritual things. They just can't see
what God has done for them.

_____

_____

_____

_____

_____

Now ask God to open their eyes so
they see He is real.

God opened the donkey's mouth
and then Balaam's eyes.

Read verses 28-35

Amazing stuff! A talking donkey!
An angel with a sword! And a
special message for Balaam from
God!

*What was God's lesson for Balaam?
Take every third letter to find out.*

THSESPELEETATTK

EROSJNUSLTSYPEWL

LHOUATGTOBIBLTEDE

YGLOOLKTYOYOOUU

S_____

_____

_____**(v35)**

Pray again!

We often say things for our own
selfish purposes. Stuff that is
ungodly. Ask God to help you to
say things that please Him — to
say the things He wants you
to say.

Read verses 36-41. Will Balaam
speak God's words? Or will he
turn against God and curse the
Israelites? Find out tomorrow...

WEIRD WORDS

Vineyards
Where grapes are
grown and wine is
made

Reckless
Careless & wrong

Summons
Being called before
the king

Sacrificed
Gave them as gifts
to fake gods

Simply the blessed

Numbers
23 v 1-26

King Balak has asked Balaam to put a curse on his enemies, the Israelites. But God told Balaam not to speak against His people. What will Balaam do?

Read Numbers 23 v 1-12

Did Balaam curse God's people (v11)?

YES/NO _____

WEIRD WORDS

Altars
Tables where offerings (gifts) to gods were put

Barren height
Somewhere high up and away from everyone

Denounce
Say things against someone

The righteous
People who live God's way

Misfortune
Bad stuff

Divination/ Omens
Evil magic and trickery

Balaam did as God said, and only spoke God's words. God would not let the Israelites be cursed (v8).

This first message from God sounds strange, but it confirms one of God's promises to Abram (we read about them two days ago!).

Read verse 10 again

> Who can count the d__ __ __ of Jacob?

Flick back to Genesis 13 v 16

> I will make your offspring like the d__ __ __ of the earth!

God kept His promise to give Abram many, many descendants!

Read Numbers 23 v 13-26

What great thing does verse 21 say about the Israelites?

> The L__ __ __ their G__ __ is w__ __ __ them

God is ALWAYS with His people. That's true for Christians today too!

Pray!

Thank God for this great blessing that He's given His people. Thank God that He is always with His people. He never leaves them!

Land of hope and glory

**Numbers
23 & 24**

King Balak is getting annoyed with Balaam because he won't curse the Israelites.

WEIRD WORDS

The Almighty
God, who is so powerful!

Fall prostrate
Fall on your face out of respect

Jacob/Israel
The Israelites

Aloes/Cedars
Plants and trees

Abundant
Loads of it!

Exalted
Made great

Read Numbers 23 v 27-30
Despite Balak's anger, God continued to speak through Balaam.

Read Numbers 24 v 1-7
God promised to take the Israelites to a beautiful land where they would have everything they needed.

*Find God's promise to the Israelites in **Exodus 3 v 8**. Then draw what you think it looked like. Use your imagination! **Numbers 24 v 5-7** gives you some help.*

As always, God kept His promise.

In the next issue of *Discover*, we'll read how Joshua led the Israelites into the amazing land of Canaan.

What else did God promise them?

Read Numbers 24 v 8-9

The Israelites would defeat their enemies. Just as God had promised (in Genesis 22 v 17).

Wow!
God always keeps His promises to His people!

Read Numbers 24 v 10-14
Balak was furious with Balaam. But Balaam still refused to speak against God.

Do you ever give in to peer pressure and speak against God or church or other Christians?

Pray!
Ask God to give you the courage to speak up for Him and never against Him.

Bye bye Balaam

Numbers
24 v 15-25

sceptre

But God hadn't finished speaking through Balaam yet.

Read Numbers 24 v 15-19
What does all that mean?

*To find out, fill in the missing words by going **backwards** one letter (B=A, C=B, D=C etc).*

King Balak was furious with Balaam, because he wouldn't put a curse on the Israelites. So Balak hit the roof and sent Balaam home.

A great _ _ _ _ _
S V M F S
will come out of Israel (v19)

He will _ _ _ _ _ _ _
D P O R V F S
Israel's enemies (v18)

Verse 17 says this king will defeat the Moabites. And God kept His promise!

Which king would lead the Israelites to victory over the Moabites and other enemies?

_ _ _ _ _
E B W J E

Check your answer in 2 Samuel 8 v 2.

But the rest of the Bible shows us that God sent a much greater king to lead His people. Who?

_ _ _ _ _
K F T V T

Wow!
God kept His promise. He sent Jesus, the greatest King ever.

When Jesus died on the cross and was raised back to life, He defeated people's biggest enemies — sin and death.

Read Numbers 24 v 20-25
The Israelites' enemies would be destroyed!

Pray!

Thank God that He always keeps His promises. Thank Him for sending Jesus to defeat sin for us! Maybe you'll find it helpful to write your prayer out. Write it as a letter to God, telling Him exactly how you feel.

Trusting God

**Numbers
26 v 63-65**

At the beginning of Numbers, Moses took a census to count the Israelites. *Flick back to Numbers chapter 1 to fill in the gaps.*

The story now moves from Balaam back to Moses and the Israelites....

**Census in the desert of

S_____

(Numbers 1 v 1-2)

Number of men in Israel's

army: _____

(Numbers 1 v 45-46)**

Just two months after this census, the Israelites reached the edge of Canaan. God had promised to give Canaan to the Israelites to live in. But the people were too scared to enter Canaan. They **didn't trust God** to defeat their enemies and give them the land.

As the punishment for not trusting God, they spent **40 years** wandering in the desert. During that time, God said that everyone who hadn't trusted Him would die.

But God took **special care** of the Israelites. During those 40 years of walking, their clothes didn't wear out and their feet didn't swell! (Deuteronomy 8 v 4)

After 40 years wandering in the desert, time for **another census**.

**Census on the p_____

of M_____

(Numbers 26 v 1-4)

Number of men in Israel's

army: _____

(Numbers 26 v 51)**

The two census totals were very similar. But the actual people were very different...

Read Numbers 26 v 63-65
All the adults who hadn't trusted God had died, except for Moses and also Joshua and Caleb, who were saved because they had trusted God.

WEIRD WORDS

Plains of Moab
Large open space in the country of Moab

Jordan
The big river they had to cross to go into Canaan

Jericho
Important city in Canaan

Pray!

Everything happened just as God had said it would. Thank God that His words always come true. Ask Him to help you trust what He has said, as Joshua and Caleb did.

Strength and courage

Deuteronomy
31 v 1-8

Next, we leap into the book after Numbers.

It's called Deuteronomy, which means **second law,** *because Moses is reminding the Israelites of God's laws for how they should live for the* **second time.**

Deuteronomy Update

• In Deuteronomy, Moses gave three long speeches just before he died.

• Moses reminded the people of the great things God had done for them.

• He urged them to continue living God's way when they went to live in Canaan.

• Why not set aside time to read what Moses said in chapters 1 to 30?

But we're going to jump to the end of what Moses told the people. Let's listen in on an important announcement...

Read Deuteronomy 31 v 1-2

How old was Moses?

Would he lead the Israelites across the Jordan into Canaan?

WEIRD WORDS

Forsake
Abandon

Read verses 3-8

Who would cross over into Canaan ahead of the Israelites?

Would God destroy their enemies?

Who had God chosen to lead the people into Canaan (v3)?

The Israelites would have a new leader. But it would be the same God who went with them!

There was no need to be afraid. God would never let them down!

Write out verse 6

If you're a Christian, that's true for you too! How cool is that? How does it make you feel?

You could make a poster of the verse and stick it on your wall.

Pray!

Thank God loads that He is always with His people, giving them the strength and courage they need to live for Him.

Stop, look and listen

Deuteronomy 31 v 9-13

Read Deuteronomy 31 v 9-13

What did Moses tell the people to do every seven years? Use the code to find out.

Why did Moses tell the people to listen to God's laws (v12)?

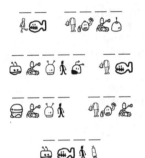

Moses has been reminding the Israelites of God's laws, to help them live God's way as they go to live in Canaan.

Moses knew how important God's law was. He knew that the people would find it hard to keep living God's way. So he wanted them to be reminded of how God wanted them to live.

WEIRD WORDS

Ark of the covenant
Special wooden box with the 10 Commandments in it (see pic above)

Feast of Tabernacles
Feast celebrating the harvest and God's goodness to His people

Wow!
We have the Bible, which shows us how God wants us to live. We should read it as often as possible, learning how to serve God. We should also listen to people who teach from the Bible — God has loads He wants to teach us!

That doesn't mean being terrified of God! It means knowing how great and powerful God is and giving Him the respect He deserves, living our lives for Him.

Pray!
Ask God to teach you loads as you read the Bible. Ask Him to give you a passion to learn more from Him and to live a life that pleases Him.

A	D	E	F	G	H	I	L	N	O	P	R	S	T	W	Y

Remember remember

Deuteronomy 31 v 14-29

God has some important things to tell Moses and Joshua.

Read Deuteronomy 31 v 14-22

> *How would the Israelites treat God after Moses died (v16)?*

Read verse 23

God reminded Joshua that he could lead the Israelites bravely because God would take them safely into Canaan.

> *What did God tell Moses to do to help remind the Israelites of what they'd done (v19)?*

Read verses 24-29

Moses told the Israelite leaders what God had said. They had no excuse for disobeying God as God had warned them so many times. But they would still continue to rebel against God.

WEIRD WORDS

Commission
Tell him how he will serve God

Prostitute themselves
Serve false gods

Forsake
Abandon

Covenant
Agreement

Thrive
Become wealthy and successful

Disposed
What they tend to do

Rebellious/ Stiff-necked
Refusing to live God's way

Corrupt
Dishonest

The Israelites would continue to disobey God. So Moses would teach the people a song to remind them of how great God had been to them and how badly they had treated God.

Wow!

Sometimes it seems as if we can't stop disobeying God.

But, amazingly, God still loves us even after we've messed up. He still helps us to fight the sin in our lives. So don't give up! He'll help us live His way more and more!

Action!

How will you remind yourself of how great God is, and that you need to keep obeying Him? Make a poster of a cool Bible verse? Make yourself a wristband? Do something!

Pray!

We can't do it on our own — we need God's help! Ask God to help you stop rebelling. Ask Him to help you with specific sin problems you have.

Songs of praise

**Deuteronomy
32 v 1-12**

God taught
Moses a song.

Let's listen in to
his warbling.

Read Deuteronomy 32 v 1-12

Moses taught this song to the
Israelites. It would remind them of
how great God was and what He
had done for them. It would also
remind them that they'd turned
against God many times (v5-6),
even though He had been so
brilliant to them.

*From each of the verses below
describe in your own words what
Moses sang about the Lord.*

> **Verse 4**

> **Verse 10**

> **Verse 11**

Action!

*Now use what you've written
down to write a song praising
God. It doesn't have to rhyme!
Tell God how you feel.*

Pray!

Now sing it or read it to God, as a
prayer, telling Him how important
He is to you.

*If you have time, read verses 13-52
for the rest of Moses' song and a
reminder that Moses wouldn't get
to live in Canaan.*

What a save!

Deuteronomy 33 v 26-29

Moses blessed the different tribes of Israel, saying something special to each of them.

You can read what he said in **Deuteronomy 33 v 1-25**. But we're going to read the very last words Moses ever said. They're about God's people — the Israelites.

Moses is near the end of his life, but he has a few more things to say...

Read Deuteronomy 33 v 26-29

The Israelites were God's special people. He protected them and destroyed their enemies, giving the Israelites a new home in Canaan.

How does Moses describe the Israelites in verse 29? Go back one letter to find out.

*Who else can be called **"a people saved by the Lord"**?*

‾‾ ‾‾ ‾‾ ‾‾ ‾‾ ‾‾ ‾‾ ‾‾ ‾‾
D I S J T U J B O T

Wow!

If you're a Christian, then you have been saved by God too. Not because you're good enough for Him. But because Jesus died to rescue you.

WEIRD WORDS

Jeshurun
Another name for the Israelites

Majesty
Great power and authority

Eternal
God lives forever

Refuge
Protection, safety

Glorious sword
God would fight for the Israelites

Their heights
Where false gods were worshipped

‾ ‾‾ ‾‾ ‾‾ ‾‾ ‾‾
B   Q F P Q M F

‾‾ ‾‾ ‾‾ ‾‾   ‾‾ ‾‾
T B W F E   C Z

‾‾ ‾‾ ‾‾   ‾‾ ‾‾ ‾‾ ‾‾
U I F   M P S E

The Israelites weren't like anyone else. They were unique. Not because they were especially good (we know they weren't!), but because they'd been **CHOSEN BY GOD**. He had saved them from Egypt.

And was now bringing them to Canaan, just as He'd promised.

Think & pray!

Moses reminded the Israelites of all that God had done for them. They should praise and thank Him — and obey His law. The same is true for you and me. If you're a Christian, thank God for saving you. Ask Him to help you to obey Him, and live His way.

For the free e-booklet *Why Did Jesus Die?* email discover@thegoodbook.co.uk or check out www.thegoodbook.co.uk/contact-us to find our UK mailing address.

Prophet loss

Deuteronomy 34 v 1-12

It's time to say goodbye to a great man of God...

When Moses had finished teaching the Israelites, he climbed to the top of a nearby mountain. From there, God showed him the whole of the promised land of Canaan.

Read Deuteronomy 34 v 1-8

Moses saw the promised land, and knew that God would bring the Israelites safely there.

But Moses didn't go with them. He died on the mountain.

Read verse 9

Who became the new leader of the Israelites?

God gave Joshua His Holy Spirit to help him make wise decisions as leader. We'll read all about Joshua and the Israelites in the next issue of *Discover*.

Read verses 10-12

FIll in the missing vowels (aeiou) to complete the description of Moses from these verses.

WEIRD WORDS

Descendants
People who would be born into their family

Grieved/ Mourning
Spent a long time showing how upset they were that Moses had died

Prophet
Messenger for God

Signs
Miracles

There has never been a pr__ph__t in Isr__ __l quite like M__s__s (v10).

The L__rd knew Moses f__ce to fac__ (v10).

God used Moses to do great m__r__cl__s in __gypt in front of Ph__r__ __h (v11).

No one had shown the m__ghty p__w__r and awesome d__ __ds (v12) that Moses did. God used Moses to do amazing things for Him!

Wow!

But God did promise to send someone even greater than Moses! **Read Deuteronomy 18 v 15-18.** That's talking about **Jesus**. God used Moses to rescue His people from Egypt. But God sent Jesus to rescue us from sin.

Pray!

Thank God for what He's taught you through Moses' amazing life. And thank Him for sending Jesus to rescue us!

THE HARDEST QUESTIONS
TO ASK ABOUT CHRISTIANITY
(AND SOME ANSWERS)

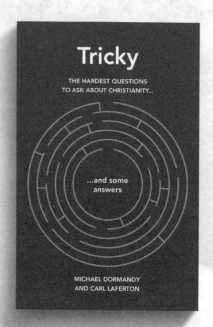

Tricky
Michael Dormandy & Carl Laferton

If Jesus is real, why is there so much suffering? Hasn't science disproved God? How can there only be one true religion?

Everyone has questions… here's a chance to think them through. This book doesn't try to win an argument, but it will show you how Jesus' answers make sense of our lives.

thegoodbook.co.uk/tricky
thegoodbook.com/tricky

HERO

When an ordinary person meets
an extraordinary God

Jonty Allcock

LOST

When the Dream turns
to a Nightmare

Jonty Allcock

FAKER

How to live for real when you're
tempted to fake it

Nicholas T. McDonald

FEARLESS

Standing firm when the
going gets tough

Jonty Allcock

DISCOVER
COLLECTION

ISSUE 9

DISCOVER ISSUE 9

March into the promised land with Joshua. Examine Luke's eye-witness evidence about Jesus. And discover the best gift EVER in Romans.

COLLECT 12 THE SET

COLLECT ALL 12 ISSUES TO COMPLETE THE DISCOVER COLLECTION

Don't forget to order the next issue of Discover. Or even better, grab a one-year subscription to make sure Discover lands in your hands as soon as it's out. Packed full of puzzles, prayers and pondering points.

thegoodbook.co.uk thegoodbook.com